Looking in the Distance

Richard Holloway was Bishop of Edinburgh and Primus of the Scottish Episcopal Church. A former Gresham Professor of Divinity and Chairman of the Joint Board of the Scottish Arts Council and Scottish Screen, he is a fellow of the Royal Society of Edinburgh. *Leaving Alexandria* won the PEN/Ackerley Prize and was shortlisted for the Orwell Prize. Holloway has written for many newspapers in Britain, including the *Times, Guardian, Observer, Herald* and *Scotsman*. He has also presented many series for the BBC television and radio; his latest book, *Waiting for the Last Bus*, originated as a five-part series on Radio 4 in 2016.

D1386934

Also by Richard Holloway

Let God Arise (1972)
New Vision of Glory (1974)
A New Heaven (1979)
Beyond Belief (1981)
Signs of Glory (1982)
The Killing (1984)
The Anglican Tradition (ed.) (1984)
Paradoxes of Christian Faith and Life (1984)
The Sidelong Glance (1985)
The Way of the Cross (1986)
Seven to Flee, Seven to Follow (1986)
Crossfire: Faith and Doubt in an Age of Certainty (1988)
The Divine Risk (ed.) (1990)
Another Country, Another King (1991)
Who Needs Feminism? (ed.) (1991)
Anger, Sex, Doubt and Death (1992)
The Stranger in the Wings (1994)
Churches and How to Survive Them (1994)
Behold Your King (1995)
Limping Towards the Sunrise (1996)
Dancing on the Edge (1997)
Godless Morality: Keeping Religion Out of Ethics (1999)
Doubts and Loves: What Is Left of Christianity (2001)
On Forgiveness: How Can We Forgive the Unforgiveable? (2002)
How to Read the Bible (2006)
*Between the Monster and the Saint: Reflections on the
Human Condition* (2008)
Leaving Alexandria: A Memoir of Faith and Doubt (2012)
A Little History of Religion (2016)
Waiting for the Last Bus: Reflections on Life and Death (2017)

Looking in the Distance

The Human Search for Meaning

RICHARD HOLLOWAY

CANONGATE

For Jeannie
Constant companion on the journey

This Canons edition published in Great Britain, the USA and Canada in 2019
by Canongate Books

Distributed in the USA by Publishers Group West and in Canada
by Publishers Group Canada

First published in Great Britain in 2004 by Canongate Books Ltd,
14 High Street, Edinburgh EH1 1TE

canongate.co.uk

1

Permissions are acknowledged on pp. 225–226

British Library Cataloguing-in-Publication Data
A catalogue record for this book is available on
request from the British Library

ISBN 978 1 78689 393 2

Typeset in Monotype Bembo by Hewer Text Ltd, Edinburgh

Printed and bound in Great Britain by Clays Ltd, Elcograf S.p.A.

Contents

Acknowledgements

Whenever I have quoted from Scripture in this book I have used the King James Bible, sometimes called the Authorised Version, though Adam Nicolson tells me it was never authorised. Anyway, after a lifetime of modern translations of the Bible, I have gone back to the King James, for two reasons. There are many Christians who claim to believe that the Bible is a contemporary or living text, a sort of running Web page from God. I never really believed that, even when I thought I did, but I certainly don't believe it now; which is why I have used a text that makes no bones about being an obviously archaic document. We are talking about the olden days here, and I think that King James makes that point obviously and without argument. But the other reason is just as important. I continue to think that the Bible, like many ancient myths, goes on bringing great wisdom to the human community, and great beauty as well. I think the splendour of the King James Bible helps to carry both of those truths.

I would also like to acknowledge my gratitude to Jamie Byng, my enthusiastic publisher, and to Mairi Sutherland, my consistently helpful editor, for all their suggestions. My warm thanks are also due to Ruth Scott for lots of good advice during the crafting of this text; and to Amy Purden for suggesting the Hafix poem to me that seems to sum up so much of what the book is about.

RICHARD HOLLOWAY
EDINBURGH, 2004

Preface

Negative Capability: that is when a man is capable of being in uncertainties, Mysteries, doubts, without any irritable reaching after fact and reason.

> *Letter of John Keats to George and*
> *Tom Keats (No. 45)*

In 1999 I wrote a book called *Godless Morality: Keeping Religion out of Ethics.* As the title suggests, the book had two aims. I set out to argue against the claim that, without religion, people would soon give up on ethics; that without God there could be no human goodness. And I sketched an outline of what a purely secular or godless ethic would look like. I tried to find good human responses to a number of contemporary ethnical challenges. The book was well reviewed in most of the secular newspapers and criticised by most of the religious press. It was praised by some philosophers and attacked by the then Archbishop of Canterbury, George Carey.

This new book is a companion volume. It attempts to do for human spirituality what *Godless Morality* tried to do for ethics. Spirituality is a notoriously difficult word to define. The word covers the inner life of human beings, all that is left when you have fed and sheltered them, and that's just about everything that is important to them. Spirituality, like morality, has been the traditional preserve of religion. Indeed, it has a whole subsection of theology to itself, covering subjects such as prayer, silence and self-discipline. But for many people today religion is no longer a way of life that is possible for them. They may or may not 'believe' in God, but they are no longer comfortable in any of the traditional religions. This enormous group of people has been described as 'the Church alumni association' or 'the Church in exile'. However, there is something faintly patronising in those descriptions. For many people in our secular society, religion has never held any attraction for them. They have not left the Church for the simple reason that they were never in it. And they do not cease to be interested in spirituality or the inner life of the human community just because they are not members of any of the religions on offer in our society. They are fascinated by the human passion for trying to understand the universe; and they admire the way science tries to look unflinchingly at the reality of things. They revel in the richness of human art and, through its various forms, they experience moments of grace and transcendence. They are increasingly fascinated by the complexities of the human psyche as revealed by the psychological study of human nature; and they are aware of the long human search for wholeness and healing. In short, there is a rich and diverse range of human spiritualities in the world, and countless people follow them without reference to religion or any necessary sense to God. I have written this book for that great company, because I now find myself within it.

The book is in four movements. The first three loosely cover some of the philosophical, psychological and ethical elements of human spirituality. The fourth is about endings, the ending of traditions and the ending of human life itself in death. Reading it over, I can see that this is a very personal book. For better or for worse, it is one man's account of what he has seen after a lifetime spent looking in the distance.

I
LOOKING

STILL LOOKING

All religions will pass, but this will remain:
simply sitting in a chair and looking in the distance.

VASILII ROZANOV

For years I have been haunted by that aphorism from Vasilii Rozanov. Indeed, I could claim to have lived its meaning in my own life. I was drawn into religion as a small boy from the back streets of an industrial town in the west of Scotland. The religion I encountered there was of the high romantic variety, heavy with incense and laden with mystery. I had no clear sense about what it meant except that it suggested heroic adventure, an endless quest after an object flying from desire. Years later I recognised myself in A.S.J. Tessimond's poem 'Portrait of a Romantic':

He is in love with the land that is always over
The next hill and the next, with the bird that is never
Caught, with the room beyond the looking glass.

He likes the half-hid, the half-heard, the half-lit,
The man in the fog, the road without an ending,
Stray pieces of torn words to piece together.

He is well aware that man is always lonely,
Listening for an echo of his cry, crying for the moon,
Making the moon his mirror, weeping in the night.

He often dives in the deep-sea undertow
Of the dark and dreaming mind. He turns at corners,
Twists on his heel to trap his following shadow.

He is haunted by the face behind the face.
He searches for last frontiers and lost doors.
He tries to climb the wall around the world.[1]

I gave my life to that search. I became a priest, then
a bishop, then a primate. Now, forty years and many
battles later, it has passed and I am left sitting in the
chair looking in the distance.

What remains is the innate compulsion to go on
asking the unanswerable question of life's meaning.
And it is the fact of its unanswerability that makes

the question so compelling. We find ourselves as
conscious beings in an apparently unconscious
universe and wonder what it means. We know quite
a lot about *how* we came about, but there is no
satisfactory explanation as to *why* we came about. I
know, of course, that many confident explanations
have been given to the question Why? The short-
hand term for one of these explanatory systems is 'a
religion', complete with indefinite article, though
the really confident ones always claim the most
definite of definite articles for themselves: theirs is
the Religion, the really true set of answers to life's
questions. Many people find one or other of these
answer systems satisfactory. They don't like living
uncertain lives with the big question permanently
unanswered, so they go for closure by opting into
one of the religions. Then they can get on with
building up the rest of their lives with that big hole
in the foundations filled in. If you can manage that
arrangement there is much to be said for it. Apart
from anything else, it can bring distinct psychological advantages. I remember reading years ago about
a well-being scale that claimed there was a distinct
correlation between faith and psychological health.

This may be why Nietzsche thought that religion evolved to help us fight depression:

> The main concern of all great religions has been to fight a certain weariness and heaviness grown to epidemic proportions . . . This dominating sense of displeasure is combated by means that reduce the feeling of life in general to its lowest point. If possible, will and desire are abolished altogether . . . The result, expressed in moral-psychological terms, is 'selflessness', 'sanctification'; in physiological terms: hypnotization – the attempt to win for man an approximation to what in certain animals is hibernation, in many tropical plants estivation, the minimum metabolism at which life will still subsist without really entering consciousness. An astonishing amount of human energy has been expended to this end.[2]

Nietzsche seems to be referring to one side of religion here, its use as a suppressant of or antidote to the nagging discontent that characterises the human species in highly developed societies. Buddhism is probably the most successful exponent of this kind of practical religion: it has little doctrinal superstructure, but it is rich in methods of self-suppression that help to purge us of those incessant desires that bite at us like wolves. Most religions retain elements of this kind of therapeutic self-culture, but many of them, particularly in the West, have also developed along heavily theoretical lines. Rather than concentrating on inculcating in their followers methods for coping with the pressures of the world, they set out to explain its meaning and origin. The trouble with the explanatory side of religion is that its theoretical usefulness is invariably of limited duration and is inevitably overtaken by the emergence of new knowledge. That is why for many people religions work for a time, then go on to lose their plausibility. The Sufi Master and poet Hafiz observed that:

> The
> Great Religions are the
>   Ships
> Poets the life
>   Boats.
> Every sane person I know has jumped
>   Overboard . . .[3]

That may be why Rozanov does not say that religion will pass, but that religions, in the plural, will pass. We may abandon particular ships, preferring the intimacy of the life-boat or the exhilaration of swimming in the sea to the routinisation of life on one of the great explanation-tankers of organised religion. But even if we choose to go overboard and swim alone, we have not necessarily abandoned the religious quest; not if we think of it as the name we give to humanity's preoccupation with its own meaning or lack of meaning. There are any number of metaphors we can use to capture this insistent concern we have about ourselves. Hafiz used the image of swimming alone in the sea, others talk about life as a search for the great unknown, Rozanov described it as looking in the distance. Following the Rozanov metaphor, I want to do a bit of distance gazing. I want to sit in the chair and describe some of the conflicting things I have seen. I shall not attempt to weave them into an explana-tory package, to make them continuous with each other. That would not be honest to my own expe-rience of the mystery of life, which has been disjunctive and contradictory rather than seamless; so I shall leave things jagged and disconnected, just as I saw them.

But before I settle myself in the chair to start describing what I see, let me affix a health warning. Religion, even without the definite or indefinite article in front of it, is dangerously volatile stuff. The root of the difficulty lies in the nature of the claims religions make about matters that are beyond any verification. This uncertainty, which lies at the heart of all religious systems, famously produces compensating protestations of absolute certainty about matters that are intrinsically unknowable. This is what gives such a dangerous edge to religious conflict. It is why Montaigne dryly observed that it was rating our conjectures highly to burn people alive for them. Another mordant observer of the excessive self-importance of religious systems was the Israeli poet Yehuda Amichai. I spent an afternoon with him in Jerusalem just before his death a few years ago. Amichai described himself as an atheist, but he was a wise and wonderfully tolerant observer of the religious madness of his own city of Jerusalem. He wrote a poem called 'Jerusalem Ecology', the first stanza of which I'd like to recite as a prophylactic against religious poisoning.

The air above Jerusalem is saturated with prayers and
    dreams
Like the air above industrial towns
it's hard to breathe.[4]

Having paid close attention to that health warning,
let me now settle into the chair and describe some of
the things I see in the distance. I propose to thread
onto a string of narrative some beads of quotation,
mainly from poets, who best capture the essence of
the human experience at those vulnerable moments
when we are most open to the mystery of our
own existence. The first one I call 'looking into the
abyss'.

Looking into the abyss

It's three o'clock in the morning and I can't sleep,
which is probably why I'm in that chair, not in bed.
I've made a pot of dark roast coffee to clear my head
and help me think, because I have been invaded by
a terrible sense of ultimate meaninglessness. I have
been engulfed by the void, made to look into the
abyss of emptiness that life seems to be stretched

upon. Everything I once thought to be steady and enduring has disappeared into the ceaseless flux of a universe without meaning. The mood is probably best expressed by Philip Larkin's 'Aubade' – dawn:

> I work all day, and get half-drunk at night.
> Waking at four to soundless dark, I stare.
> In time the curtain-edges will grow light.
> Till then I see what's really always there:
> Unresting death, a whole day nearer now . . .

What unnerves Larkin is not the thought of a wasted life, the quite natural remorse many of us appropriately feel as we look back on our lives:

> – The good not done, the love not given, time
> Torn off unused –

No, what frightens him is extinction, complete nothingness, non-being. He is overcome by a sense of

> . . . the total emptiness for ever,
> The sure extinction that we travel to
> And shall be lost in always. Not to be here,

Not to be anywhere,
And soon; nothing more terrible, nothing more true.

This is a special way of being afraid
No trick dispels. Religion used to try,
That vast, moth-eaten musical brocade
Created to pretend we never die,
And specious stuff that says No rational being
Can fear a thing it will not feel, not seeing
That this is what we fear – no sight, no sound,
No touch or taste or smell, nothing to think with,
Nothing to love or link with,
The anaesthetic from which none come round.
And so it stays just on the edge of vision,
A small, unfocused blur, a standing chill
That slows each impulse down to indecision.
Most things may never happen: this one will . . .[5]

As far as I am concerned, Larkin has captured the
mood all right, but not exactly the object of the
anxiety. My blues in the wee small hours are not
caused by apprehension at the prospect of my own
death and extinction, though I hope my number will
not be called any time soon. No, my mood is more
universal than that. It is a puzzled revulsion at the
pointless plenitude of Being, and dismay at the way

this planet has manufactured trillions of life forms only to cast them indifferently aside, like an out-of-control assembly line in an old Charlie Chaplin movie. My mood of nihilistic despair is amplified by the thought that most of these lives have known enormous pain and the human ones considerable sorrow, if only at the end when life itself slowly undermines them before withdrawing completely. The mood of early morning loss comes from a sense of bafflement at the massive indifference of the universe. We try to care about one another, but life itself, the life that impels its indifferent way through time and space, does not seem to care about anything; it simply is. Even that does not quite capture the mood, because to say that the life force that activates the universe 'is' gives it a sense of stability, when, in fact, we experience it as constant change; it is not so much Being, as Passing, as something endlessly in the process of becoming something else. There are times when the cosmic indifference of life is as disorienting as being lost in a dense wood or as frightening as falling overboard into the sea at night with no one to know we have gone.

The strange thing is that this void, this Nothing or

No one, gave us birth, and it is impossible not to be emotionally involved with a parent, however absent and indifferent. There's a poem that captures this ambiguity better than the straightforward despair of Larkin's 'Aubade'. I am thinking of 'Psalm' by Paul Celan. Celan was a poet of the abyss, a victim of the brutal indifference of history. His parents were lost in the Nazi death camps and he himself, like other Holocaust survivors, committed suicide. He wrote a wrenching series of poems called *Die Niemandsrose*, 'The No one's Rose'. This is one of them:

> No one moulds us again out of earth and clay,
> no one conjures our dust.
> No one.
>
> Praised be your name, no one.
> For your sake
> we shall flower.
> Towards
> you.
>
> A nothing
> we were, are, shall
> remain, flowering:

the nothing–, the
no-one's-rose.

With
our pistil soul-bright,
our stamen heaven-ravaged,
our corolla red
with the crimson word which we sang
over, O over
the thorn.[6]

The thorn wound over which we sing is perplexity at our own being, which we cling to as the mysterious gift it is; but who is there to praise for the gift?

Sensing an absence

Who is there to praise for the gift of life? It is now six o'clock in the morning and the city is beginning to wake up. I brew more coffee and get back into the chair. The mood has changed. Celan has softened Larkin's bleak nihilism and restored a sense of latency to the scene, a sense of something undisclosed, something absent that might once have been present. Wistfulness rather than despair is the mood now. I call this six-o'clock-in-the-morning mood 'sensing an absence'. And it is God who is absent. The sense of the absence of God is strong in Europe at the moment. I am not talking on behalf of confident secularists for whom God has never been present. For them the universe has been thoroughly disenchanted, even disinfected, purged of any residue of that disturbing presence. And I am obviously not talking about confident believers for whom God is still on tap. No, I am talking about those who find themselves living in the No Man's Land between the opposing forces of confident unbelief and confident belief. Those of us who are living Out There in the place where God is absent are deafened by the clash of claim and counter claim, as the rival explanations are fired over our heads. It is important to say that Out There is not a place of neutral agnosticism. It is a place of committed unknowing. Those of us in this place of unknowing believe that the war of opposing interpretations is pointless, because the mystery of the meaning of Being can be neither demonstrated nor destroyed by explanation, it is a wound that has to be endured. And R.S. Thomas is our poet:

Why no! I never thought other than
That God is the great absence
In our lives, the empty silence
Within, the place where we go
Seeking, not in hope to
Arrive or find.
He keeps the interstices
In our knowledge, the darkness
Between stars.
His are the echoes
We follow, the foot prints he has
Just left.[7]

It is because we love the honest poverty of the state of unknowing that those of us who are Out There also believe in the moral importance of atheism. But for us atheism is not a straightforward noun, a fixed state of final explanation. It is a verbal noun, *atheising*, a dynamic process that constantly tries to rid the mind of conceptual idols because it understands the cruelty of idols and their need for constant warfare. Of course, atheism itself can become a conceptual idol, a fixed position as belligerent as theism, which is why evangelical atheists and evangelical theists could be said to deserve each other. 'God' is the term we have devised to signify, however hypothetically, the ultimate causal agent of a universe whose existence remains stubbornly unexplained. But the secret history of humanity's relationship with God is a story of abandonment – our abandonment of God and God's abandonment of us, leaving only the echoes of previous attempts at explaining the mystery. This constant work of separating ourselves from earlier understandings of God is morally essential if we are not to trap ourselves in a cave worshipping projections of our own shadows. This is the truth behind the eastern imperative: 'If you meet the Buddha on the road kill him.' It is the truth that lies behind the Hebrew fear of idolatry, which is the substitution of a knowable object for the unknowable mystery of God.

Living in this state of unknowing about the ultimate meaning or unmeaning of things is so arduous and painful that it is entirely understandable that we constantly create theoretical objects for ourselves onto which we project a fictitious reality in order to rescue us from uncertainty. The classic text on the subject is from the Book of Exodus, at the beginning of chapter 32:

And the people gathered themselves together unto Aaron, and said unto him, Up, make us gods, which shall go before us; for as for this Moses, the man that brought us up out of the land of Egypt, we wot not what is become of him. And Aaron said unto them, Break off the golden earrings, which are in the ears of your wives, of your sons, and of your daughters, and bring them unto me. And all the people brake off the golden earrings which were in their ears, and brought them unto Aaron. And he received them at their hand, and fashioned it with a graving tool, after he had made it a molten calf: and they said, These be thy gods, O Israel, which brought thee up out of the land of Egypt.

Like the Israelites who were frustrated by Moses' long absence, we do not enjoy the state of waiting. For most people, waiting is the prelude to something else, it is never a state of mind in its own right. We are always waiting *for* something, which we anticipate patiently or impatiently. For those of us who are living in the absence of God, waiting is not anticipatory; waiting is its own meaning, it is a permanent state of unknowing. But this way of being is counter-intuitive to our normal needs and desires. We want answers, explanations, portable idols. This is the attraction of all explanatory systems. It accounts, for instance, for the current appeal of a Christian education course called Alpha, which gives briskly confident answers to all of life's puzzling questions.

If we could stop the flow of human knowledge and experience, and if Being itself were not in a constant state of passing or becoming, these systems might attain a satisfying perfection, a resolution which is very attractive to the religious temperament. That is why some religious communities completely opt out of the flow of history and locate themselves, as they might put it, *in* but not *of* the world, so that their perfectly realised religious system is protected from the erosions of time. Amish Christians and Hasidic Jews are examples of communities that have chosen to enclose themselves in a time capsule rather than trust themselves to the unpredictable torrents of change. But those religious communities that decide to take their chance in history are constantly overtaken by the incessant flux of events. Most of the big religions that are active today have been around for millennia. Many of their explanatory claims were forged in ancient societies, which were very different from our own. To take an obvious example, they all tend to accord to women a status of fixed subordination to men. There may have been good reasons why the subordination of women was appropriate when it was originally religiously codified, but it makes little sense in developed societies today.

Dramatic examples of the painful tensions that ancient religious traditions can create for contemporary human beings are provided by stories in the recent news, from Iran, England and the USA. In June 2003 the newspapers told us that the Audrey Hepburn look was all the rage among young women in Iran. They liked to wear chic headscarves wrapped under the chin and trendy shades. They enjoyed sitting at sidewalk cafés, drinking coffee and smoking cigarettes, just like Audrey Hepburn in her first big movie break, Roman Holiday, in 1953. The Islamic clerics who run the country denounced and vainly tried to forbid this unseemly behaviour in young women because it was clearly in defiance of traditional Islamic practice.

Clerics, of whatever persuasion, are rarely happy with social and cultural change. The difficulty they always face when they confront a challenge to established social relations is what to do about the sacred scriptures upon which their particular system is based, particularly if the new developments promote change in the status of women and the understanding of human sexuality. Another example of this tension, expressed this time through Christianity, was the row that broke out in England and the USA in the summer of 2003 over the proposed appointment of two gay men as Anglican bishops. Traditionalists noisily opposed the appointments on the grounds that the Bible condemned homosexual relationships, while supporters pointed out that the writers of the Bible did not have our contemporary understanding of homosexuality. The bullying tactics of the traditionalists prevailed in England and, after several weeks when he was rarely off the front pages of the world's newspapers, the priest in question was forced to withdraw. In the USA, however, the Church authorities confirmed the election of a gay man as a bishop, and he was subsequently ordained, though the row that surrounds his appointment is likely to continue indefinitely within the Anglican Church.

The Bible and the Koran were written thousands of years ago, so they naturally reflect the human arrangements and understandings of their time. This is why the flux of history is tough on clerics who believe that everything in their scriptures is permanently commanded, including male dominance and homophobia, because it means they have to apply first- or seventh-century customs to twenty-first-century men and women, who, not surprisingly, don't much care for them.

It is the idea of God behind these ancient ways of organising society that is the main source of difficulty, because God is always claimed as the basis for the enduring authority of the systems that are under siege. Traditional religions have a picture of God as a superhuman person, possessing absolute power over us, who inhabits a heavenly realm that is separated from the earth, but is in regular contact with it, the way NASA communicates with its space stations. Many people find the NASA model for God, as a supernatural engineering and maintenance agency, very difficult to hold today. Religion used to claim with considerable cogency that, given the intricacy of our nature and the way we are precisely adapted to the universe, a great external intelligence had to have designed it all. It was expressed by William Paley in the famous 'lost watch' argument in 1802. If you found a watch when you were out walking and marvelled at the perfect intricacy of its design, you would correctly deduce that it had been created by a watchmaker. So it was with the universe itself, the argument went. The idea of God the Designer offered an explanation for the way species seemed to be so miraculously adapted to the world in which they found themselves. That explanation worked for centuries, until Darwin came along with an alternative account that was truer to the facts and therefore more satisfying. He showed that we were not the result of a straightforward piece of planned engineering, but of an unimaginably long and painful process of trial and error through which successful species gradually adapted themselves to their environment. The process was hit-and-miss and intrinsically wasteful, completely unlike the precisely designed economy of the religious explanation. According to Martin Rees, 'fewer than ten percent of all the species that ever swam, crawled, or flew are still on Earth today'.[8] Richard Dawkins called one of his books *The Blind Watchmaker* to make a similar point.

Apart from a few defiant creationists, most people in the West today have abandoned the old argument from design. What is now left of the explanatory use of God to account for the organised intricacies of planet earth has retreated to one of the last frontiers of human knowledge, which is the human mind. Religious explainers now try to tell us that the mind inhabits the brain, but is not reducible to it. This is sometimes called the Ghost in the Machine theory: the idea that our bodies, though they are physical mechanisms, are inhabited by an invisible spiritual reality called mind or soul, exactly in the way that God is understood to inhabit and direct the universe. This is a development of Plato's idea that fundamental reality is spiritual and immaterial, but that it assumes the form or appearance of matter in actual entities, the way the Invisible Man in the old movie would sometimes wrap himself in bandages and pop a pipe in his mouth so that people could locate his presence. The significant thing about the appearances was that they were mere shadows of heavenly realities and had no enduring life of their own; only the spiritual had enduring life. Applied to individual humans, this gave us the idea that our bodies are temporary habitations for our souls, and when the body dies the soul returns to its immortal state.

What gave this theory such a long run was the

experience of our own consciousness. We seemed to ourselves to be more than material realities. Our mind was an invisible power that transcended our bodies, so it was easy to believe that it had an independent and separate existence that would outlast its house of clay. By extension, God was understood as the Super Mind or Spirit that activated the created universe but was independent of it. As is the way of these things, this theory, the last frontier of defensive religion, quickly becomes the next frontier of science, and Antonio Damasio, a leading neuroscientist, is one of its explorers. In his book *Looking for Spinoza*,[9] Damasio explores the mind/brain question from a philosophical as well as a scientific angle. He offers an account of the way evolution has endowed us with a complex neural system that enables us to regulate our life in a way that maximises well-being and minimises pain. He tells us that those neural reactions of pain or pleasure we call 'feelings' were built from simple responses to external events that promoted the survival of the organism. Feelings are brain states, whether of fear or compassion, that prompt us to respond to our environment in ways that will be conducive to our own safety and flourishing. The mind is not some sort of self-existent ghost that temporarily inhabits our flesh; it is a way of describing how the brain expresses our bodies. But, as I have already pointed out, because of the way we experience ourselves as somehow transcending our bodies, it is easy to understand how we were led to posit the idea of a self that existed independently of its physical container. That assumption about ourselves is strengthened by the fact that the gift of memory enables us to recognise patterns in our experiences, thereby giving us some level of control over our instinctive responses to the pressures that beset us. And by enabling us to unify our own remembered history, however inaccurately, the experience of memory lends force to the tendency to abstract ourselves from the brain that has so intelligently organised our experiences for us. The tragic disproof of the claim that there is a fundamental essence in us that is independent of the body is clearly demonstrated in cases where assaults to the physical brain change or utterly destroy the personality or selfhood of the person, long before their body as a whole has died. We could apply to these tragic people some of the words from Larkin I have already quoted – 'nothing to think with, Nothing to love or link with'.

Damasio's investigations force us to reappraise some of the most vexing philosophical problems that have haunted us since the emergence of consciousness. Are we controlled by a separate reality, whether it is God in the case of the universe or the mind in the case of ourselves, or are the structures of both the universe and the mind explicable in terms of themselves without reference to outside forces? Darwin gave us a way of understanding the evolution of life on earth without the necessity for an external agency to guide its development. Damasio offers us a parallel explanation of the mind that is hopeful as well as convincing. The fact that it is hopeful is interesting. One of the many charges that retreating religionists make about the explanatory advance of science is that, by reducing everything to biology, it leaves no ground for a satisfying spirituality or an authoritative ethic for humanity. However, scientists increasingly argue that nature itself provides the best basis for ethics because it prompts us to live prudently and to care for one another, as well as for the earth on which we live, if we want to survive and flourish. This is a theme that I shall develop in a later section of this book. Damasio even offers us a naturalistic account of human spirituality. He writes:

> I assimilate the notion of (the) spiritual to an intense experience of harmony, to the sense that the organism is functioning with the greatest possible perfection. The experience unfolds in association with the desire to act toward others with kindness and generosity. Thus to have a spiritual experience is to hold sustained feelings of a particular kind dominated by some variant of joy, however serene. The center of mass of the feelings I call spiritual is located at an intersection of experiences: Sheer beauty is one. The other is anticipation of actions conducted in 'a temper of peace' and with 'a preponderance of loving affections.' These experiences can reverberate and become self-sustaining for brief periods of time. Conceived in this manner, the spiritual is an index of the organizing scheme behind a life that is well balanced, well-tempered, and well-intended. One might venture that perhaps the spiritual is a partial revelation of the ongoing impulse behind life in some state of perfection. If feelings testify to the state of the life process, spiritual feelings dig beneath that testimony, deeper into the substance

of living. They form the basis for an intuition of the life process.[10]

It is the life process, the encounter with Being itself, that is becoming the focus for human spirituality and ethics today. Traditional religious explanations for the mystery of life, which were entirely understandable in their time, projected the significance of life beyond itself to a supernatural self-existent reality that was believed to have called life into existence and upon whom life was permanently dependent. This binary theory of reality inevitably downgraded the significance of the world itself, because it was held to be a rival to its creator; and it projected the credit for humanity's best discoveries and insights onto this imagined distant authority. Christianity, without entirely understanding what it was doing, tried to balance the record by claiming that God in Christ had become immanent in the world, and had embedded himself in human nature. At the same time, it tried to retain the traditional idea that God was also entirely separated from and transcendent to the world. This is the basis for its claim that Jesus Christ was completely man and completely God at the same time. Contemporary secular spirituality finishes the process that was begun in Christian theology, by severing humanity from its dependence on a supposed external supernatural authority. We seem to be living through a time in which one part of humanity is beginning to claim autonomy or self-governance for itself and to acknowledge that meaning now has to be discovered in the life process itself. We may be no closer to understanding why there is a world, but we are now able to accept the fact that the world itself is the source of the values and meanings we prize most, not some hypothetical transcendent reality which did none of the work yet claims all the credit. One way to express this is to say that the spirit is now engendered by and encountered in the world in which we find ourselves. Rather than positing an external force to account for our most cherished experiences, we begin to understand how they were generated within us in response to the life process itself. And it is through us that the universe has become aware of this. This is mystery enough to be going on with, without hanging on to ancient hypotheses that now create more problems for us than they solve.

Intrigued by the strangeness of it all

But after six uncomfortable hours in the chair, I need more than another coffee break; I need something to take my mind off the dizzy contemplation of the mystery of Being. By nine o'clock in the morning I am being stunned by the serious weirdness of the universe. I once asked a couple of distinguished scientists what was happening before the Big Bang. That, they said, was the $64,000 question no one could answer, though it did not stop people from trying. The fact of the universe, of why there is something and not just nothing, is puzzling enough; what is even more baffling is that through us the universe is now asking questions about itself. One wit inverted that way of putting it, by saying that a physicist is the atom's way of thinking about atoms. We have not yet encountered other conscious agents in the universe capable of generating questions about their own meaning and the nature of the reality in which they find themselves, but given the vast scale of the universe it is likely that they are out there somewhere. Astronomers tell us that there may be as many as 140 billion galaxies in the visible universe. Bill Bryson offers an analogy to help us get our minds round that unimaginable number. He suggests that if galaxies were frozen peas there would be enough of them to fill the Royal Albert Hall.[11]

Apart from its impossible vastness, the more we think about it, the more weird our knowledge of the universe and our place within it becomes. Our mathematicians, those prodigies who inhabit a sphere of pure reason, do their calculations and, years later, we discover that the discernible processes of the universe correspond exactly to their mental equations. That the human mind can put us in touch with the intricate structure of the universe is intriguing enough; the emergence of humanity itself is an even more tantalising story. The fact that after 15 billion years our planet became a home for self-conscious beings is worth meditating on, though I am not sure where it gets us. Scientists tell us that our emergence into conscious life is the consequence of certain finely tuned elements called anthropic balances. If the earth were a little closer to the sun it would be too hot for life and if it were a little further away it would be too cold. If the orbit of the earth were slightly different then life on earth would never have emerged. It is the precise balance of two great forces that creates the right conditions for life to exist. The expansive force of the Big Bang spreads the universe out, while the contractive force of gravity pulls it back together. If the gravitational force were too high, the universe would appear, but in a microsecond gravity would pull everything back into a Big Crunch. If the expansion rate were too high, then the universe would stretch at such a rate that gravity would be unable to form the stars and galaxies from whose dust carbon-based life evolved. The chances of these conditions being precisely satisfied are as likely as those of shooting at a target an inch square on the other side of the universe and hitting it. These delicate adjustments do not only refer to the earliest instance, but to the continuing history of the world and its detailed processes.

This extraordinary fine tuning appears to be necessary at every stage of world development. So it is no surprise that religious thinkers point to these anthropic balances as new and compelling evidence for an element of cosmic design. We have already seen that one of the traditional arguments for God was the argument from the appearance of design in nature to the existence of a transcendent designer. We have also been cautioned by the way science has consistently overtaken these hypotheses that posited the existence of an external creation agency and shown us how the life process explains itself from within. That will almost certainly happen with the fine tuning of the universe and the anthropic balances, as well. Scientists already offer a number of ways of explaining them without reference to an external engineer, including the possibility of multiple universes in time/space. Martin Rees believes that there may be an infinite number of universes and that we simply exist in one that combines things in a way that enables us to exist. He offers the analogy of a clothing store: 'If there is a large stock of clothing, you're not surprised to find a suit that fits. If there are many universes, each governed by a differing set of numbers, there will be one where there is a particular set of numbers suitable to life. We are in that one.'[12]

But what about the fact of the existence of the life process itself? If we take it simply as it is in itself without reference to any supernatural originating agency, what kind of reality is the huge, many-sided fact of Being? If what we already know about the universe is anything to go by, the answer may not be to our liking. That's certainly what the poet Robinson Jeffers suggests in his poem 'The Great Explosion':

> The universe expands and contracts like a great
>   heart.
> It is expanding, the farthest nebulae
> Rush with the speed of light into empty space.
> It will contract, the immense navies of stars and
>   galaxies, dust-clouds and nebulae
> Are recalled home, they crush against each other
>   in one harbor, they stick in one lump
> And then explode it, nothing can hold them
>   down; there is no way to express that explosion; all
>   that exists
> Roars into flame, the tortured fragments rush away
>   from each other into all the sky, new universes
> Jewel the black breast of night; and far off the
>   outer nebulae like charging spearmen again
> Invade emptiness.
>   No wonder we are so fascinated with fire-works
> And our huge bombs: it is a kind of homesickness
>   perhaps for the howling fire-blast that we were
>   born from.

But the whole sum of the energies
That made and contained the giant atom survives. It
    will gather again and pile up, the power and the
    glory —
And no doubt it will burst again; diastole and systole:
    the whole universe beats like a heart.
Peace in our time was never one of God's promises;
    but back and forth, die and live, burn and be
    damned,
The great heart beating, pumping into our arteries
    His terrible life.

                    He is beautiful beyond belief.
And we, God's apes — or tragic children — share in the
    beauty.
We see it above our torment, that's what life's for.
He is no God of love, no justice of a little city like
    Dante's Florence, no anthropoid God
Making commandments: this is the God who does
    not care and will never cease. Look at the seas
    there
Flashing against this rock in the darkness — look at the
    tide-stream stars — and the fall of nations — and
    dawn.
Wandering with wet white feet down the Carmel
    Valley to meet the sea. These are real and we see
    their beauty.

> The great explosion is probably only a metaphor – I
> know not – of faceless violence, the root of all
> things.[13]

Anger at the cruelty of it all

The spectacle is certainly magnificent and draws forth
awe from us, as we contemplate the implacable
momentum of the life-power that surges indifferently through the universe. This was certainly why
Nietzsche admired the raw honesty of the warrior
aristocrat before the Church weakened his tough
ethic with Christian pity. 'The essential characteristic
of a good and healthy aristocracy is ... that it accepts
with a good conscience the sacrifice of untold human
beings who, *for its sake*, must be reduced and lowered
to incomplete human beings, to slaves, to instruments.'[14] There is a terrible honesty in that. It is the
raw unconscious honesty of the lion who trails the
herd of antelope and picks off the wounded straggler
with beautiful ferocity. It is possible to admire the
fierce symmetry of the balance between species in
nature and to understand why, for example, the
orphaned baby elephant has to be ignored by the rest

of the herd and left to die. The species cannot afford
to care for the individual, only for its own survival.
But one's heart winces at the sight, and feels that it
should not be this way among humans. There is something in us that seems to be emotionally reluctant to
abandon the stragglers who limp behind the human
herd. That is why we respect and occasionally support
those who work to help the wretched humans of the
earth and to succour the wounded who cannot keep
up with the pace of the strong.

The interesting thing to notice here is that the
great champions of those who are reduced to slaves
or instruments of the strong are probably more
motivated by anger than by pity. This is a mysterious
phenomenon: a universe born in violence and driven
by remorseless power gives birth to beings who are
made angry by the very law of life, by the structure
of the universe that gave them life. That's why my next
mood, my noonday mood, is best described as 'anger
at the cruelty of it all'. For me, the best model of this
anger is Jesus; not the divinised Christ who was co-
opted by the powerful to sit in distant splendour
above the chancel arch in vast cathedrals, but the
human Jesus, the angry prophet of Nazareth. Over the

years I have been as guilty as any preacher of making him in my own image or of doctoring him to suit my own needs. But once we abandon the salvation scheme that sees him as a divine figure sent to rescue us from God's wrath at our God-inflicted sinfulness, we get him back in a way we may not really want. He becomes the fiercest exemplar of the Hebrew tradition of the prophets, that group of men who were angered by the way the powerful drove their chariot wheels over the wretched of the earth. This is high anger at the very order of things, but it is particularly aimed at those upon whom the arbitrary indifference of the universe may be said to have smiled, yet who take their good fortune as evidence of their own virtue or rightful place in the scheme of things:

> Woe unto you that are rich! For ye have received your consolation. Woe unto ye that are full! For ye shall hunger. Woe unto ye that laugh now! For ye shall mourn and weep.[15]

These words were uttered by Jesus at a time when the distance between the rich man and the destitute peasant was no vaster than the gulf which now exists between a Californian billionaire and the child of a crack addict in one of the LA ghettoes. Jesus knew that the poor were always going to be with us, but he despised the religious theorists who offered divine justification for the insensate cruelty of it all. He seems to have had some respect for the Romans who governed his country, probably because they did not try to offer any kind of theological justification for their imperial ascendancy. Their confidence lay in their own power, which they delighted in exercising. The powerful of our era lack the blunt honesty of the Nietzschean warrior who roared like a lion and rejoiced in his strength for its own sake. The powerful today try to make a virtue of their arbitrary good fortune, justify it by theory, *explain* it. And religion has consistently offered its services as the Great Explainer in Chief. This accounts for Jesus' anger at religion, seen at its most torrential when he drove the money-changers out of the temple, because they were symbols of the way religion was used to deepen the misery of the poor by exploiting their piety for gain:

> And Jesus went into the temple, and began to cast out them that sold and bought in the temple, and

overthrew the tables of the moneychangers, and the seats of them that sold doves; and would not suffer that any man should carry any vessel through the temple. And he taught them saying, Is it not written, My house shall be called the house of prayer? But ye have made it a den of thieves.[16]

Jesus belonged to that tiny group of men and women in history who instinctively ally themselves with the victims of power. Their spiritual psychology is explained very simply in a novel about one of the worst political crimes of the twentieth century, the genocide in Rwanda in 1994. Gil Courtemanche, in *A Sunday at the Pool in Kigali*, puts these words into the mouth of Gentille about her lover Bernard Valcourt, a Canadian journalist:

I know exactly why I love you. You live like an animal guided by instinct. As if your eyes are closed and your ears are blocked, but there's a secret compass inside you that always directs you to the small and forgotten, or impossible loves, like ours. You know you can't do anything, that your being here won't change a thing, but you keep going anyway.[17]

People like Bernard are not able to do much about the way the small and forgotten are constantly crushed by the powerful, apart from occasionally snatching a victim from the advance of the juggernaut. But they are able to bear witness against the ugly cruelty of power and the people it corrupts. They become recording angels whose words stand defiantly against the evils they protest. In the dangerous work of being the voices of the universe's victims they frequently end up as victims themselves, but their death then becomes part of their testimony and it is remembered long after their persecutors are forgotten.

While it is true that many of these prophetic figures emerge from religion, the defiant side of religion is invariably compromised by its own collusion with power and its compulsive need to explain why things are the way they are. Institutional religion has not only developed theories to justify political power and social privilege as specifically ordained by God, it has even sought to justify the pain of non-human creation, usually along the lines that God knows best how to run a universe and who are we to challenge his methods? It is precisely at this point that many people hand back the ticket, leap overboard from religion and take to the empty sea. This was what Darwin did, oppressed by what he called the clumsy, wasteful, blundering, low and horridly cruel works of nature. In a frequently quoted letter to Asa Gray, written in 1860, Darwin says:

> I cannot persuade myself that a beneficent and omnipotent God would have designedly created the Ichneumonidae with the express intention of their feeding within the living body of caterpillars.[18]

He was referring to the fact that these enterprising wasps sting their prey not to kill but to paralyse them, so their larvae can feed on fresh (live) meat.

But theoretical religion is probably at its most repellent when it tries to explain the arbitrary suffering that suffuses human history, particularly when it justifies God's role in it all, usually as the helpless architect of human freedom. This is why some of the most principled and compassionate people in history have proclaimed that if there is behind the universe that which we call God, an almighty originating authority, then no human being should attempt to justify its ways or have anything to do with it. Instead, like Ivan Karamazov in Dostoevsky's great novel, they should simply return the entrance ticket and try to dissociate themselves from such a cosmic abuser of power:

> Tell me honestly, I challenge you – answer me: imagine that you are charged with building the edifice of human destiny, whose ultimate aim is to bring people happiness, to give them peace and contentment at last, but that in order to achieve this it is essential and unavoidable to torture just one little speck of creation, that same little child beating her breasts with her little fists, and imagine that this edifice has to be erected on her unexpiated tears. Would you agree to be the architect under these conditions?[19]

Ivan Karamazov's anger was provoked by the torture of a single child, yet what is that compared with the monumental sorrow of all the lost and blighted children of history, not to mention the humdrum miseries of ordinary mildly afflicted humans? Alas, rather than remain silent in the face of such overwhelming sorrow, the Church has blitzed humanity with explanations for suffering. I was inoculated against them as a young curate when, for the first time, I conducted a child's funeral. It was a bleak day in early February and we buried him in a cemetery streaked with dirty snow on a hillside in Lanarkshire. The father, wearing his Sunday suit, carried the little white coffin in his arms, and we threw earth on to it and I spoke words into the wind. Afterwards I tried to comfort the young mother, who was tight with grief and anger, by attempting a consoling explanation of her loss. She turned on me fiercely and thrust me away from her. She did not want her honest anger polluted by my religious explanations. How could she not be consumed with raging grief at the death of her only son?

That kind of anger is still the most honest response to the victims of the indifferent power of the universe. And yet the emergence of that anger is itself a mystery. How did a universe, born of explosive power, give birth to this angry pity for the victims of that same power? There is no answer to the question. It is part of the mystery of unknowing that wounds us. But, though there is no answer, we should not leave the matter there: we should let our anger beget a compassion that goes against the cruel grain of the

universe. It is well expressed in a poem by Sylvia
Townsend Warner called 'Road, 1940':

> Why do I carry, she said,
> This child that is no child of mine?
> Through the heat of the day it did nothing but fidget
>   and whine.
> Now it snuffles under the dew and the cold star-
>   shine,
> And lies across my heart heavy as lead,
> Heavy as the dead.
>
> Why did I lift it, she said,
> Out of its cradle in the wheel-tracks?
> On the dusty road burdens have melted like wax,
> Soldiers have thrown down their rifles, misers slipped
>   their packs;
> Yes, and the woman who left it there has sped
> With a lighter tread?
>
> Though I should save it, she said,
> What have I saved for the world's use?
> If it grow to hero it will die or let loose
> Death, or to hireling, nature already is too profuse
> Of such, who hope and are disinherited,
> Plough, and are not fed.

But since I've carried it, she said,
So far I might as well carry it still.
If we ever should come to kindness someone will
Pity me perhaps as the mother of a child so ill,
Grant me even to lie down on a bed;
Give me at least bread.[20]

The sudden, inexplicable kindness of strangers is the best thing in the universe and it is uniquely human. It is a break in the order of nature that tells us, with cold ruthlessness, that in times of terror and calamity each of us is bound to save ourselves and leave the world's wounded to perish. Yet, throughout our history, there have always been those who have made these defiant challenges against the pitiless order of things. Never many, of course, but enough to disturb and influence the rest of us and rouse us occasionally to action. The French novelist Albert Camus understood our reluctance to get involved, but he also knew that, in the end, some people do act. At the end of his novel *The Plague*, we hear him meditating:

Dr Rieux resolved to compile this chronicle, so that he should not be one of those who hold their peace but should bear witness in favour of those plague-

stricken people; so that some memorial of the injustice and outrage done to them might endure; and to
state quite simply what we learn in time of pesti-
lence: that there are more things to admire in men
than to despise. None the less, he knew that the tale
he had to tell could not be one of a final victory. It
could be only the record of what had had to be done,
and what assuredly would have to be done again in
the never-ending fight against terror and its relent-
less onslaught, despite their personal afflictions, by
all who, while unable to be saints but refusing to
bow down to pestilences, strive their utmost to be
healers.[21]

Camus' Dr Rieux was not motivated by religion in
his work of healing. But to be fair to Christianity, the
religion I know best, down the ages it has produced
countless people who have followed the way of Jesus
in serving the poor and trying to heal the world.
Christians are still to be found in the worst places on
earth, trying to make a difference to the lives of the
wretched. It is in its work of organised care for others,
whatever its theological basis, that Christianity is at
its most compelling. Secular spirituality is at a disad-
vantage here. Because it is diffused throughout society

rather than separately organised within it, it is more difficult to get it engaged in systematic and coordinated methods to change society. The problem is not that there is a lack of purely secular bodies dedicated to human welfare and the mending of the world; it is that there is no obvious agency that can gather the godless together to motivate them for the work. There is, of course, a host of agencies in the form of campaigning organisations and highly committed individuals, but the godless don't gather together once a week to be ethically challenged and spiritually uplifted. There have been attempts in the past by secular enthusiasts to copy the methods of the great religions and apply them to purely worldly purposes, but they were never very successful and have declined more dramatically than the Churches whose techniques they sought to copy. If the medium is the message, then it may be that secular spirituality will make a virtue of its diffused state, since it reflects humanity in its current situation, where community is increasingly something that is chosen rather than something that is given. Nevertheless, there are unifying instruments available to the committed that constitute a virtual community, such as the Internet, which was extensively used in mobilising opposition to the Iraq War, and which can be used to gather the new spiritual diaspora together on a functional basis whenever it is needed. Another increasingly significant gathering point for the human community is provided by music, which offers to its disciples not only moments of grace and transcendence but also opportunities for protesting against the excesses of the powerful. So it could be argued that the lack of any single organising authority is itself an important mark of contemporary human spirituality; and that the specific occasionality of its coming together is one of its most important strengths.

Encountering presence in absence

The day is wearing on. It is late and a kind of peace has come over me. It is the peace that comes from accepting a duty, but before I try to define it I have to describe the almost final mood of the day. I call it 'encountering presence in absence'. I can no more explain it than I can account for the experience of the abyss. All I can say is that, as well as moments of deep emptiness, the mystery of Being affords us

fleeting moments of encounter with what feels like a
kind of presence. To be more exact: it feels like the
presence of the great absence in our lives that leaves
only echoes or footprints. We have to be careful not
to turn these moments into religious objects, to reify
them into explanatory idols. They are, anyway, beyond
description. It is impossible to find verbal equivalents
for them, to catch them in words. Poetry comes clos-
est to communicating the mystery of the experience.
I want to quote a poem about one of these encounters. It came to that remarkable woman Simone Weil,
who refused ever to board any of the ships of religion
that ply their wares on the oceans of human sorrow
and uncertainty. It is by Edward Hirsch and it is called
'Simone Weil in Assisi':

> She disliked the miracles in the gospels.
> She never believed in the mystery of contact
> here below, between a human being and God
> She despised popular tales of apparitions.
>
> But that afternoon in Assisi she wandered
> through the abominable Santa Maria degli Angeli
> and happened upon a little marvel of Romanesque
>   purity where St Francis liked to pray.

> She was there a short time when something absolute
> and omnivorous, something she neither believed
> nor disbelieved, something she understood – but what
> was it? – forced her to her knees.[22]

I have had one or two moments like that in my life. Because of my religious background, I was always tempted to interpret them as evidence for the official claims of Christianity. Now I am happy just to let them be. They are as much a part of the human experience of the mystery of Being as the experience of nothingness and the abyss. We do not need to posit any supernatural agency to account for them. They are intrinsic to the life process and can be explained in natural terms. Nevertheless, they come to us as sheer gift, as an encounter with the graciousness of Being, as a kind of exultation in the pure fact of living. It is their very ordinariness that makes them significant. At the very least they help us stop trying to explain life and they prompt us to start living it with a bit more passion and gratitude. I'll end this movement with a description of one I had that comes very low down the Richter scale of mystical experience. Nevertheless, the commonplace experience I am going to recount was a moment of grace.

It was well after ten on a late June evening. I was driving back to Edinburgh from North Berwick, which is about twenty miles east of the city on the edge of the North Sea. It was one of those clear-as-day nights we get in Scotland in midsummer, when it never really gets dark. I could see across the Firth of Forth to Fife and the mountains of Perthshire beyond. I had the car window right down so that I could smell the poppy-studded hayfields lining the road. On the car radio Holst's *Planets* was being broadcast in a concert and they'd just got to the Jupiter theme. Suddenly, my right arm was out of the window and I was shouting 'Yes' to no one. I felt that if my life had contained only that moment, the brief visit of a mayfly, my time would have been justified. Early in the morning I had asked myself who there was to praise for the mystery of Being. Here I was at the end of the day simply giving thanks to the perfumed Scottish night, saying 'Yes' to the absence that felt like a presence. It was enough.

A kind of defiance

It is at moments like that that I find myself confronted by a certain gracious latency in creation, a sense of something not yet disclosed. Is there something in the life process itself that is trying to express itself through the dark mirror of human consciousness? Obviously, there is no way of answering that question, but there is a way of responding to it. We could choose to live as though the best meaning and purpose we can find for our own lives is the very meaning and purpose of the universe itself. We could pay the universe a compliment it probably does not deserve by living as though its purpose were love, as one tradition in Christianity says it is. And if the universe, in the end, were to prove us wrong, who cares? Our lives, then, would have been an act of defiance of indifferent power, and power is always worth defying. Even though we experience God as absent, we should continue to live as though he were present in love. That's why I love the old Castilian romantic, Miguel De Unamuno. In his great book *The Tragic Sense of Life* he quotes these words: 'Man is perishing. That may be; and if it is nothingness that awaits us let us so act that it will be an unjust fate.'[23]

II
SPEAKING

2

TELLING TALES

The Cleves loved to recount among themselves even the minor events of their family history . . . because these family discussions were how the Cleves made sense of the world. Even the cruelest and most random disasters – the death, by fire, of one of Charlotte's infant cousins; the hunting accident in which Charlotte's uncle had died while she was still in grammar school – were constantly rehearsed among them, her grandmother's gentle voice and her mother's stern one merging harmoniously with her grandfather's baritone and the babble of her aunts, and certain ornamental bits, improvised by daring soloists, eagerly seized upon and elaborated by the chorus, until finally, by group effort, they arrived together at a single song; a song which was then memorized, and sung by the entire company again and again, which slowly eroded memory and came to take the place of truth.[1]

DONNA TARTT

You would expect a novelist as accomplished as Donna Tartt to rate the telling and embellishing of stories as one of the most significantly human things that we do. It's a bit more surprising to come across a scientist who claims that story-telling is deeply rooted in human biology; but that is the claim made by Stephen Jay Gould, a great American scientist and baseball addict. In a book published a few weeks after his death, he wrote these words:

> The vertebrate brain seems to operate as a device tuned to the recognition of patterns. When evolution gifted consciousness in human form upon this organ in a single species, the old inherent search for patterns developed into a propensity for organizing these patterns as stories, and for explaining the surrounding world in terms of the narratives expressed in such tales.[2]

I cannot offer any intelligent response to Professor Gould's claim that our propensity for creating stories is biologically determined, but I am in no doubt that telling stories about ourselves is the most characteristically human thing we do. Like the Cleve family in Donna Tartt's novel, story-telling is the way we try to make sense of the world, and we seem to have been doing it since we started to speak. All communities have developed family narratives about themselves; that is why the best way to understand a society is to explore its stories. In this movement, I want to think about the two big stories we have told to explain ourselves in the West, the kind of stories that philosophers call grand narratives, great sweeping accounts of who and what we are.

The first thing to notice is that the stories we tell about ourselves can conflict with each other. Passionate protagonists for a particular story arise, who claim that we have to make a choice and pick their account, their explanatory narrative, if we are to conform to the truth of things. This adversarial approach, though dramatic, is too simple. The meaning behind the big stories we tell about our-selves is much more complex and subtle than this take-it-or-leave-it attitude suggests. There is always more to our tales than the rehearsal of disputable facts. Charles Freeman[3] points to an ancient dis-tinction in the status of the stories we tell. When the Greeks wrote about science or mathematics, or any other factual discipline, they called their text a *logos* or reasoned account. The word they used, from which our words 'logic' and 'logical' come, came to take on the meaning of reasoned thought, factual knowledge, something close to what we mean by science today, though we'll soon see that even science can slide into the other kind of story we tell ourselves. The Greeks called this second kind of story *muthos*, from which our word 'myth' comes. The classic example of its use were the stories the Greeks told about their gods. That's why it is easy to jump to the wrong conclusion here and assume that myths are false, because they concern unreal fantasies, while reasoned narratives are true, because they are about real facts. It would be more accurate to say that each kind of story can be true in different ways. The contrast between fiction and non-fiction may help here. A written fiction, such as a great novel, may not be true in the purely factual sense – the characters do not exist in real time – but it can be a carrier of profound spiritual and psychological truth. Strictly speaking, the distinction between *muthos* and *logos*, myth and a reasoned, factual account of anything, is not absolute. Factual, historical events, such as great battles or revolutions, can become the founding myths of a nation in a way that transcends the purely factual reality of what happened. Most people would accept that, but it may be more controversial to suggest that even scientific accounts of reality can become mythic in their scope and assume an almost religious importance for their proponents. I suspect one of the major thinkers of the twentieth century would agree with me.

I am talking about Thomas Kuhn, author of *The Structure of Scientific Revolutions*, one of the most influential texts of the twentieth century. Kuhn was invited to teach a course on the history of science to humanities students at Harvard in the 1960s. He discovered in his research that the picture he had in mind of the development of science was not quite in line with what actually happened. He had an idea of it as a cumulative, linear process that ate its way into the facts of the universe, rather like one of those machines that munch into a seam of coal in an underground mine. There is undoubtedly much truth in that characterisation of science. It does accumulate factual knowledge about the universe; and when it genuinely discovers things they usually stay discovered. Science is clearly an incremental discipline that accumulates provable facts about the universe, such as the precise boiling temperature of water. But at the broader interpretative level Kuhn discovered that the progress of science was much more dramatic and interruptive than the process of gradually acquiring new facts would suggest. He used the phrase 'paradigm shift' to express the revolutionary way it actually operated. The scientific community developed a working paradigm, a constellation of beliefs, assumptions and techniques, which was the prevailing account of reality in a particular community at a particular time. The important thing to notice about these paradigms was that, in addition to being a summation of current scientific knowledge, a list of accumulated hard facts, they were active, working constructs. They did more than describe how things were; they were operationally useful. They enabled the human community to understand and manipulate its external environment, both practically and theoretically, until they could no longer do the job for which they were created, and a new systematised version of scientific knowledge, a new story, displaced them. These paradigm shifts were always hard fought, the old paradigm holding on as long as it could, partly out of ordinary caution and conservatism, partly out of the scientific ethic of ruthlessly testing new theories till they proved themselves.

The classic example of a paradigm shift in science is the move from Aristotelian to Copernican astronomy. According to the classical world view, the cosmos was a series of concentric circles, with the earth stationary at the centre. The planets moved round the earth in perfect spheres and there was nothing beyond them except the realm of God. A Christianised version of Aristotelian astronomy was an important part of the big story in Europe for centuries till, after a struggle, it was succeeded by the Copernican paradigm, which placed the sun, not the earth, at the centre of our system. I want to suggest that just because we have now replaced that old world view with a different model it would be wrong to describe the classic story as false or untrue. It was overtaken by other discoveries, just as its Copernican successor would be overtaken when its turn for relegation came, but it was honestly and appropriately held in its day. Moreover, it was practically useful; it did what it needed to do at the time. The great Egyptian astronomer Ptolemy, who worked in Alexandria between AD 127 and 141, based his work

on earlier astronomical observations, but improved
them through the use of the armillary astrolabe, the
classical skeleton celestial globe, made of metal rings,
revolving on an axis within a wooden horizon. This
enabled him to plot the position of stars more accu-
rately than earlier methods had allowed. Charles
Freeman points out that sharing, as he did, the conventional astronomical wisdom that the sun moved
round the earth, 'he was forced to come up with
extraordinarily complicated models of circles whose
own centres moved round other circles'.[4] Even
though his central assumption was wrong, I am told
that today it is still possible to navigate a ship using
the Ptolemaic map of the heavens. So we can say that
for certain purposes classical astronomy still works. I
want to use that idea of usefulness or workability as
a way of salvaging some human meaning from the
clash of narratives that we are living through today,
and which I shall spend the rest of this movement
exploring. Bearing in mind the ancient distinction
between *muthos* and *logos*, myth and reasoned argument, I shall want to suggest that, in our search for a
new human spirituality, the mythic content of
ancient religious stories can still be useful to us, so

long as we don't make the mistake of claiming a factual or rational status for them. That said, I want to turn now to the great Christian myth that has had such a profound impact on Europe and, through colonisation, on the rest of the world.

The Christian epic

Though it is fading rapidly as a working narrative among thinkers today, the story that dominated European consciousness until recently was the great drama of Christianity. Its exit has left an enormous gap in our self-understanding, though it takes a story teller rather than a historian to measure the impact of its loss. This is how John Updike sees it:

> Modern fiction . . . thrives on showing what is not there: God is not there, nor damnation and redemption, nor solemn vows and the sense of one's life as a matter to be judged and refigured in a later accounting, a trial held on the brightest, farthest quasar. The sense of eternal scale is quite gone, and the empowerment possessed by Adam and Eve and their early descendants, to dispose of one's life by a single defiant decision. Of course,

these old fabulations *are* there, as ghosts that be-devil our thinking.[5]

As Updike suggests, the Christian story explained everything, the inner and spiritual cosmos, as well as the outer or physical cosmos. Compared with the great scientific narrative that prevails today, its original version was limited, almost cosy, in its account of time and space. The famously learned James Usher, who became Archbishop of Armagh in 1625, calculated that the moment of creation was on 23 October in the year 4004 BC, which is just over 6,000 years from the present day. So in the classic version of the Christian epic we are dealing with a manageable story line. The best tales are always about someone, and this story was about Us. The earth might have been at the heart of the concentric circles of the cosmos, but it was really only constructed as a stage prop, a backdrop to the human drama. We were the purpose of the cosmos, the reason God created it. He wanted creatures who would love him and enjoy him forever. Later embellishers of the story would describe with great eloquence how God, though entirely perfect and self-sufficient in himself, wanted to create beings who would be like him, made in his own image, so that he could love them and be loved by them in return. Love that is not offered freely is not love, of course, so the story went on to describe how we were given the dangerous gift of freedom in order to freely choose to love God – or not. We were offered a choice: either an eternity of innocent happiness with God or the dangerous knowledge of good and evil that might separate us from God and catapult us into pain and sorrow. Who would not rebel against such a demanding and overwhelming parent? Which of us would not flee from such omnivorous love? According to the story, we did flee. The unknown authors of the Book of Genesis might have provided the synopsis, but it was Milton who wrote the full screenplay in *Paradise Lost*. He wrote:

> Of Man's first disobedience, and the fruit
> Of that forbidden tree, whose mortal taste
> Brought death into the world, and all our woe,
> With loss of Eden.

The narrative of the Fall in the third chapter of Genesis suggests that the emergence of sexual desire was the consequence of our primal disobedience and, for the first time, Adam and Eve realised they were naked. Later Christian thinkers radically revised the original version and claimed that it was sex itself that was the cause of all our woe and the constant means whereby our parents' guilt was passed on to humanity throughout time. Death, the other great theme of the story, was another consequence of our original disobedience. Whatever kind of interpretative gloss you put upon their story, the authors of Genesis, like good proto-Freudians, tried to account for the fact that death and sex are the two great preoccupying realities of the human condition. They wrote a timeless allegory about our mysterious capacity for destroying our own happiness by making wrong choices, yet they also tacitly acknowledged that these choices were determined by factors that were never really under our control: 'And the Lord God said unto the woman, What is this that thou hast done? And the woman said, The serpent beguiled me, and I did eat.' But it was God who created the serpent that seduced Eve. This ancient story sets forth the human dilemma: we feel guilty about the things we do, yet something in us refuses to accept full responsibility for them, because we feel we are determined by factors beyond our control, including the ineluctable fact of our own inherited nature. This is the human predicament that God has to rescue us from. There is a hint from the beginning, still echoed in some of the ancient Christian liturgies, that God, like all good writers, did not want the story of his true love for us to run smoothly, though it was to conquer all in the end. One ancient hymn talks about human sinfulness as a *felix culpa* or 'happy fault', because it gave God the opportunity to show the rocklike and unconditionally forgiving love he had for us. However we describe the human condition, whether divorced from God by our own culpable infidelity or forced into separation by a pre-ordained destiny we never could escape from, we were banished from Paradise and now wander in the land of lost content. Milton describes the great expulsion in these words:

> They looking back, all th' eastern side beheld
> Of Paradise, so late their happy seat,
> Wav'd over by that flaming brand, the Gate
> With dreadful faces throng'd and fiery arms.
> Some natural tears they dropped, but wiped them
>   soon;

The world was all before them, where to choose
Their place of rest, and Providence their guide;
They hand in hand with wandering steps and slow
Through Eden took their solitary way.[6]

Like the members of the Cleve family in Donna
Tartt's Southern Gothic novel, Christian thinkers
have added complex embellishments to the simple
narrative of our expulsion from Paradise. Not only
did it make us wanderers in a strange land, we also
became fugitives from divine justice, born guilty of
our first parents' sin:

All of us, therefore, descending from an impure seed,
come into the world tainted with the contagion of
sin. Nay, before we behold the light of the sun we
are in God's sight defiled and polluted. 'Who can
bring a clean thing out of an unclean? Not one,' says
the Book of Job. We thus see that the impurity of
parents is transmitted to their children, so that all,
without exception, are originally depraved. The
commencement of this depravity will not be found
until we ascend to the first parent of all as the foun-
tain head. We must, therefore, hold it for certain,
that, in regard to human nature, Adam was not
merely a progenitor, but, as it were, a root, and that,

accordingly, by his corruption, the whole human race
was deservedly vitiated.[7]

That is the voice of the great Protestant reformer John
Calvin, but we find an identical message in Catholic
Christianity. Here is an ugly echo of the same doctrine from John Eudes, a French Catholic saint of the
seventeenth century:

> it is a subject of humiliation of all the mothers of the
> children of Adam to know that while they are with
> child they carry within them an infant . . . who is the
> enemy of God, the object of his hatred and maledic-
> tion and the shrine of the demon.[8]

Listening to that kind of obsessive self-hatred, it
should come as to no surprise to us that the perfect
internalisation of the Christian story, in time, produced humans who were capable of gross and systematic cruelty to one another in the name of the
vengeful God who haunted their imaginations.

Having been totally corrupted by that fateful act
of disobedience and expelled from Paradise as a consequence, the story goes on to describe our long

sojourn in the country of exile, separated from God and at war with each other. The account of the expulsion from Eden, however amplified in our consciousness by Milton's great poem, is based upon the Hebrew text of Genesis, though Christianity had a particular way of interpreting its meaning. Like storytellers everywhere, Christianity has a genius for appropriating elements of other people's traditions, which it then stitches into a patchwork pattern of its own devising. It is not necessarily dishonest in doing this, but it is undoubtedly expressing its strong sense of superiority over other religious systems. It claims to be a unique instrument which God has used to communicate his final purpose to humanity. His purpose was to save us from the terrible consequences of that original choice; his method was a cumulative process of self-revelation in which the clues he scattered and the hints he dropped were finally collected into the perfect salvation narrative in the person of Jesus, who became known as the Christ, or the One Anointed by God to save us. According to this strand of the story, the tales the Hebrews told about their special relationship with God were only half understood by them. It was as though they were unconscious vehicles of God's will, chosen by him to point to truths that lay beyond their limited ability to comprehend, but which would be correctly interpreted by his new favourites in the Christian Church.

Theologians developed a technical vocabulary to describe this mysterious selection process, the simplest idea being that the Hebrew scriptures, especially the magnificent prophetic books, which had been written in response to specific historical circumstances, were actually coded predictions by God of his plans for the distant future. The most dramatic of these embedded oracles is found in Isaiah chapter 7 verse 14: 'Therefore the Lord himself will give you a sign; Behold, a virgin shall conceive, and bear a son, and shall call his name Immanuel.' These words were probably uttered by the prophet Isaiah about 700 years before the birth of Jesus. At the time, they were meant to stiffen the backbone of a frightened King of Judah, who was being invaded by his northern neighbours. Christianity claimed that these words had actually been placed by God in the Hebrew scriptures as a secret message for future readers who would be given the insight to understand them. Correctly interpreted, they provided evidence that God had made careful long-term plans to bring salvation to the whole human race. The words in Isaiah pointed ahead to the day when God would embed himself in humanity by being born of a virgin, in order to save us from our sins.

That is why some contemporary theologians describe the gospel narratives in the New Testament as not so much history remembered as prophecy historicised. One way to watch this process at work is to look at an old Bible and note the way it has been cross-referenced. For instance, if I look at Matthew chapter 2, verse 15 in my copy of the King James version of the Bible I read: 'And he was there till the death of Herod: that it might be fulfilled which was spoken by the prophet, saying, Out of Egypt have I called my son.' In the margin this verse is cross-referenced to Hosea chapter 11, verse 1. When I look this up I find it written: 'When Israel was a child, then I loved him, and called my son out of Egypt.' Matthew clearly wants us to interpret Jesus as the successor to and fulfilment of the old Israel. Just as God called the Israelites out of slavery in Egypt through the ministry of Moses, so he is now calling his children out of the slavery of sin through the ministry of Jesus. Just as importantly, God planted clues to his intentions in books written hundreds of years before the birth of Jesus Christ. To understand the imaginative stretch required by this theory, a possible comparison would be if the evangelists of New Labour in Britain were to claim that certain verses written by Geoffrey Chaucer in *The Canterbury Tales* at the end of the fourteenth century were actually secret prophecies of the birth of Tony Blair in 1953.

As with all ancient narratives, the metaphors and allusions in the fully developed Christian story mix and multiply in a gloriously inconsistent way. Sometimes humans are described as helpless slaves who need to be rescued, so God goes undercover to effect their release. He hides himself among the disregarded poor in order to dupe the enemy, the fallen angel who rules the land in which they are exiled. This is similar to one of the most colourful myths to emerge from the 2003 war in Iraq, where, according to one version of the story, Private Jessica Lynch was rescued by daring American soldiers from an Iraqi hospital. Deemed incapable of freeing ourselves, nothing is expected of humans in the great hostage recovery raid of redemption. God alone is capable of saving us, through a costly struggle on the cross with the forces of evil who had captured us. But another way of telling the story claims that humanity's fall from grace was our fault from the very beginning, and if we don't cooperate this time we will be abandoned by God forever. God seems to be no more consistent or predictable than any other parent, so it is not surprising that his children are neurotic and confused and tell stories about themselves that flit constantly between smug omnipotence and dangerous self-hatred. These unresolved tensions have never left the story that Christian theology continues to tell itself: sometimes it exhorts us to work out our own salvation by right belief and purity of life; sometimes it warns us that we have no power within ourselves to help ourselves, but that God will save us out of his absolute and unconditional love for us; sometimes it tells us that God only plans to save those whom he has chosen, irrespective of any good or evil they have done, solely on the basis of his sovereign will.

An example of the kind of paranoia that the dark confusions of the Christian story can produce in the kind of anxious people William James described as 'sick souls' is found in one of Scotland's greatest novels, *The Private Memoirs and Confessions of a Justified Sinner*, by James Hogg, a self-educated shepherd from the Borders region. Hogg, a contemporary of Sir Walter Scott, was born in 1770 and died in 1835. *Confessions* was published in 1824.

Before looking at the novel, I want to say something about the theological background that is fundamental to its meaning. One of the strangest tricks we humans play is the way we craft narratives about ourselves that turn back and abuse us, so that we end up being oppressed by our own creations. A psychological explanation for this would be to say that we project our fears and anxieties into theories that then assume authority over us, much in the way that the monster created by Dr Frankenstein avenges himself against his creator. This is what seems to happen when we create sacred texts. Stories are handed on to us from our misty past. Because of their antiquity and mysteriousness we begin to revere them. While they are in the fluid, oral stage they are not too dangerous, but once they are written down they begin to assume absolute authority over us. This is certainly what happened to the 'religions of the book' – Judaism, Christianity and Islam. In each of these ancient religions, though less so in Islam than in the other two, believers are in permanent dispute with each other about the precise authority the sacred books ought to have over their lives today. Hogg's novel is a good example of the dangers inherent in understanding religious stories not as myths that illuminate the darkness and confusion of human history but as authoritative, legal texts that command our literal obedience.

The 'justified sinner' of Hogg's story is Robert Cowan, the second son of the Laird of Dalcastle, a young man who comes to believe that he has been predestined by God to eternal salvation, irrespective of how he behaves. This vocabulary comes to us from St Paul, who seemed to teach that our eternal destiny is not determined by the way we live, but by the pre-ordained will of God. Here are the relevant verses from his Letter to the Romans, chapter 8, verse 28:

> And we know that all things work together for good to them that love God, to them who are the called according to his purpose. For whom he did fore-know he also did predestinate to be conformed to the image of his Son, that he might be the firstborn

among many brethren. Moreover whom he did pre-
destinate, them he also called; and whom he called,
them he also justified; and whom he justified, them
he also glorified. Who shall lay any thing to the
charge of God's elect? It is God that justifieth. Who
is he that condemneth?

Like many obscure verses in the Bible, these words
have been a hunting ground for fanatics for centuries.
They gave rise to the doctrine of predestination, the
idea that before they were born, God chose some
humans for salvation and others for eternal damnation. I have already quoted John Calvin on the state
of original sin we are born in, because of the fateful
choice our parents made in the Garden of Eden. This
is how he goes on to express the related doctrine of
predestination:

By predestination we mean the eternal decree of
God, by which he determined with himself whatever he wished to happen with regard to every man.
All are not created on equal terms, but some are pre-
ordained to eternal life, others to eternal damnation;
and, accordingly, as each has been created for one or
other of these ends, we say that he has been predes-
tinated to life or death.

We say, then, that Scripture clearly proves this much,
that God by his eternal and immutable counsel
determined once for all those whom it was his pleasure one day to admit to salvation, and those whom,
on the other hand, it was his pleasure to doom to
destruction.[9]

This doctrine gave rise to a consequent theory, called
'antinomianism', which held that since they had
already been inoculated against damnation by the
sovereign will of God, the elect could behave any way
they liked. It formed a prominent part of Calvinist
thinking in Enlightenment Scotland. Robert Burns –
another near-contemporary of Hogg's – captured the
whole mad business in his poem, 'Holy Willie's
Prayer':

> O Thou, wha in the heavens dost dwell,
> Wha, as it pleases best thysel',
> Sends ane to heaven and ten to hell,
>> A' for thy glory,
> And no for ony guid or ill
>> They've done afore thee!
>
> I bless and praise thy matchless might,
> Whan thousands thou hast left in night,

> That I am here afore thy sight,
> > For gifts an' grace,
> A burnin' an' a shinin' light,
> > To a' this place.[10]

In Hogg's novel, apart from Cowan's cruel rejection by his legal father, two influences have worked upon him. The first is the fanatical Robert Wringhim, the local Calvinist minister, an ardent predestinarian, who may actually be his natural father. Wringhim steeps him in the obsessive intricacies of predestinationist theology. A key passage in understanding the evolution of the lonely and insecure young man into the confused monster he becomes follows upon Wringhim's announcement that he has received assurance from God that his stepson is indeed among the predestined elect:

> From that moment, I conceived it decreed, not that I should be a minister of the gospel, but a champion of it, to cut off the enemies of the Lord from the face of the earth; and I rejoiced in the commission, finding it more congenial to my nature to be cutting sinners off with the sword, than to be haranguing them from the pulpit, striving to produce an effect,

which God, by his act of absolute predestination, had for ever rendered impracticable. The more I pondered on these things, the more I saw of the folly and inconsistency of ministers, in spending their lives, striving and remonstrating with sinners, in order to induce them to do that which they had it not in their power to do. Seeing that God had from all eternity decided the fate of every individual that was to be born of woman, how vain was it in man to endeavour to save those whom their Maker had, by an unchangeable decree, doomed to destruction. I could not disbelieve the doctrine which the best of men had taught me, and toward which he made the whole of the Scriptures to bear, and yet it made the economy of the Christian world appear to me as an absolute contradiction. How much more wise would it be, thought I, to begin and cut sinners off with the sword![11]

Cowan's darkly comic logic is fortified through the agency of a mysterious tempter called Gil-Martin, who persuades him that God's elect have been liberated from conventional moral restraints precisely in order to perform his cleansing work. Gil-Martin is a Gaelic name for a fox, and there is no doubt that Hogg wants us to recognize him as the devil, the great deceiver of humankind, who can appear as an angel of light and an instrument of God. Under the twin influences, therefore, of a deranged religious ideology and satanic seduction, Robert stumbles into his murderous career, by the end of which he has killed five or six people. But he remains a troubled and suicidal man throughout, who finally kills himself in despair, taking his satanic alter ego with him. Though *Confessions* is a dark and disturbing story, it is also very funny and nowhere funnier than in the account of the great Auchtermuchty preaching. Auchtermuchty, a small town in Perthshire, is gripped by religion:

There was nought to be heard, neither night nor day, but preaching, praying, argumentation, an' catechising in a' the famous town o' Auchtermuchty. The young men wooed their sweethearts out o' the Song o' Solomon, an' the girls returned answers in strings o' verses out o' the Psalms.[12]

Into this town, one sabbath, comes a stranger, like the avenging preacher played by Clint Eastwood in the movie Pale Rider, 'clothed in a robe of black sackcloth, that flowed all around him, and trailed far behind, and they weened him an angel, come to exhort them, in disguise'. The inhabitants of Auchtermuchty are electrified by the stranger's preaching from a text in Ezekiel:

'I will overturn, overturn, overturn it; and it shall be no more, until he comes, whose right it is, and I will give it him.' From this text he preached such a sermon as never was heard by human ears, at least never by ears of Auchtermuchty. It was a true, sterling, gospel sermon – it was striking, sublime, awful in the extreme. He finally made out the IT, mentioned in the text, to mean, properly and positively, the notable town of Auchtermuchty. He proved all the people in it, to their own perfect satisfaction, to be in the gall of bitterness and the bond of iniquity, and he assured them, that God would overturn them, their principles, and professions; and that they should be no more, until the devil, the town's greatest enemy, came, and then it should be given unto him for a prey, for it was his right, and to him it belonged, if there was not forthwith a radical change made in all their opinions and modes of worship.[13]

The narrator reminds us that 'Nothing in the world delights a truly religious people so much as consigning them to eternal damnation', so they hang upon the preacher's every word. What saves the town from the perdition to which the satanic visitor is leading it is not the sophistication of the local intelligentsia, who are all seduced by his eloquence, but the simple decency of an uneducated old man, Robin Ruthven. When his words of warning against the dark arts of the preacher are scornfully rejected by the town, he persuades them by a simple ruse:

> Robin Ruthven came in amang the thrang, and, with the greatest readiness and simplicity, just took haud o' the side an' wide gown, an' in sight of a' present, held it aside as high as the preacher's knee, and behold, there was a pair o' cloven feet! The auld thief was fairly catched in the very height o' his proud conquest, an' put down by an auld carl. He could feign nae mair, but gnashing on Robin wi' his teeth, he dartit into the air like a fiery dragon, an' keust a reid rainbow our the taps o' the Lowmonds.[14]

Hogg, through the words of the old wife of one of the weavers of Auchtermuchty, draws the moral for us:

> whenever you are doubtfu' of a man, take auld Robin Ruthven's plan, an' look for the cloven foot, for it's

a thing that winna weel hide; an' it appears whiles where ane wadna think o't. It will keek out frae aneath the parson's gown, the lawyer's wig, and the Cameronian's blue bannet; but still there is a golden rule whereby to detect it, an' that never, never fails.[15]

As I shall show in the next movement, what the old wife of Auchtermuchty called the golden rule will turn out to be of fundamental importance in the development of a purely human spirituality. Meanwhile, we should note that over the years the Christian story has produced many split personalities, such as Hogg's justified sinner, though it might be closer to the truth to say that it has provided us with a vocabulary with which to describe our already divided natures. However we account for it, the three-act drama of Christianity – banishment from Paradise, long captivity behind Enemy lines, rescue and restoration by God – has created some fascinating psychological types. It has manufactured personalities of great integrity and self-discipline who are eager to cooperate with their own salvation. It has produced personalities of staggering hypocrisy who, incapable of achieving the high standard to which Christianity called them, but unable to admit it to themselves, live lives of duplicity and denial. Other dualities worth noting include the sense of purpose that many have achieved through their confident following of the Christian way, compared with the sense of exclusion that has been induced in more transgressive personalities who were never able to conform to the pattern of expectation that was laid upon them. Christianity has produced moral clarity and direction for some fortunately straightforward people; and secrecy and self-loathing for more complex personalities. Transgressive minorities, in both the intellectual and the moral sense, have never been at ease in the Church, because the untidy reality of their actual lives constantly fails Christianity's strict quality control standard.

The most punishing version of this occurs when individuals become convinced that their inherited nature has provoked their banishment from Paradise. Incurably ill, they find themselves in a system that orders them to get well. That is why, from the beginning, people with incurably questioning minds, as well as awkward women and sexual non-conformists

have all clashed dissonantly with the official authorities of Christianity. And it is probably why there has
been such a strong streak of spiritual and physical
cruelty throughout the history of the Church.
Though it has championed charity, Christian history
has been constantly marked by cruelty, right down
to Ireland's Magdalene Laundries for unmarried
mothers and the gay witch-hunts of our own day. If
you believe in the connection between human
anguish and high art, it is not surprising that a
religion that has produced so much pain has also
produced great art, particularly great fiction. What a
religious pulp writer once called the 'Greatest Story
Ever Told' has produced some of the greatest stories
ever written, though, as John Updike has reminded
us, there is a dearth of them today. That is because the
great narrative of Christianity has been replaced, as a
working paradigm, by the great narrative of science.

The scientific epic

Today's scientific story differs from the Christian story
in almost every way. For one thing, the time frame
has shifted unimaginably. Rather than Archbishop

Usher's manageable 6,000 years, we now have to get our minds onto a time line that began 14 or 15 billion years ago with the Big Bang. This earth, the centre and purpose of the cosmos in the previous paradigm, is now described as a tiny fragment of stardust, probably about 5 billion years old, in a back street of one small galaxy in a universe of billions of galaxies. We are told that though life on earth emerged 3.5 billion years ago, our human ancestors only diverged from chimpanzees a mere 5 million years ago. Instead of being the hero of the narrative from the beginning, our species appeared on the scene comparatively recently, anything between half a million and 34,000 years ago. And far from having a divinely ordained purpose and direction, the whole thing seems to be in a permanent state of Heraclitan flux, a vast and meaningless explosion of energy that is prodigal in its indifferent wastefulness. Nietzsche, who announced the death of the Christian story over a century ago, said that 'Becoming aims at nothing and achieves nothing.'[16] The paradox is that, being gifted and afflicted with consciousness, we pay close attention to the universe, even though it is uninterested in us. We are creatures with a passion for discovering the meaning of things who find ourselves in a universe without any discernible purpose.

So what now can be the basis for human values? If there is no ultimate meaning, how do we find proximate meaning for our lives? This is what Updike was getting at when he said that modern fiction thrives only on showing what is *not* there. The practical difficulty we face is how to live harmoniously with each other within the empty spaces of the quantum universe. We would probably all agree that because of what Eliot described as the 'undisciplined squads of emotion'[17] in the human psyche, we need systems of self-control, ways to restrain our undisciplined desires. In the days of the Christian story, the main guarantor of restraint was fear; but if the complex and contradictory scheme of divine retribution no longer convinces us, what can replace it as a motive for the moral life? Many contemporary novels wrestle with this question. One of the most disturbing is Michel Houellebecq's dystopian French fiction, *Atomised*, which paints a picture of human beings shuttling helplessly between a sterile rationality and an unsatisfiable hedonism. *Atomised*, whose implicit subtext comes from Dostoevsky's famous cry, 'God, if you do not exist, then everything is permitted,' tells the story of two half-brothers, Bruno and Michel, children of a hippy mother who was completely uninterested in their upbringing. Michel is a scientist who gives up his research into the human genome in order to make time for thinking. If Michel represents the human struggle to make sense of existence in a world without ultimate meaning, Bruno represents the force of appetite in a world from which all restraint has been banished. If we classified them according to the famous Nietzschean dualism, Michel would be the classic Appollonian rationalist, Bruno the Dionysian hedonist. In Freudian categories, Michel stands for the ego, Bruno for the id, in a humanity from which the super-ego or conscience has been replaced by a moral vacuum. Michel does not seem to be interested in sex at all, while Bruno is not really interested in anything else. His life becomes a sexual odyssey, during which he makes a stop at a hippy holiday commune, the Lieu du Changement, where Tantric Zen, a combination of vanity, mysticism and frottage, is practised by New Age pilgrims whom he despises – but it's an easy way to get laid.

One of the encounters between the brothers

defines the problem faced by humans who live in our kind of scientific post-religious society. They are at the hospital where the mother who deserted them is dying:

> 'She just wanted to be young, that's all . . .' said Michel, his voice tired now, and forgiving. 'She wanted to be with young people, certainly not her kids, who just reminded her that she was part of an older generation. It's not difficult to understand. I want to go now. Do you think she'll die soon?'
>
> Bruno shrugged his shoulders. Michel got up and went into the other room; the grey-haired hippie was on his own now, peeling organic carrots. He tried to talk to him, to find out what the doctor had actually said, but the old beggar could only come up with vague details that were completely off the subject. 'She was a radiant woman . . .' he said emphatically, carrot in hand. 'We think she's ready for death, she's reached an intense level of spiritual awareness.' What the fuck did that mean? There was no point in getting into it. It was obvious the old guy wasn't actually saying anything, he was just making noises with his mouth. Michel turned on his heel and went back to Bruno. 'Fucking hippies . . .' he said as he sat down again, 'they're still convinced that religion is some sort of individual experience based on

meditation, spiritual exploration and all that. They don't understand that it's just a purely social thing about rites and rituals, ceremonies and rules. According to Auguste Comte, the sole purpose of religion is to bring humanity to a state of perfect unity.'

'Auguste Comte yourself!' interrupted Bruno angrily. 'As soon as people stop believing in life after death, religion is impossible. If society is impossible without religion, which is what you're saying, then society isn't possible either . . .'[18]

Bruno has a point. The threatening certainty of what Updike described as 'a later accounting, a trial held on the brightest, farthest quasar'[19] in a reckoning after death was one of religion's strongest cards. Except in conservative religious circles, it is a belief that has largely vanished from our society. Houellebecq is probably correct in identifying its absence as the most powerful factor in the erosion of religion in our day. But it has left a vacuum. There can be little doubt that the most powerful effect of the abandonment by society of any overarching meaning in life, of the sort that religion once gave it, is the sense of homelessness and strangeness it can provoke in us. The title of Houellebecq's book says it all: we are atomised. Like colliding billiard balls, there is little to hold us together, no common identity that can integrate us into community and its responsibilities. Indeed, this lack of a common purpose is said to be the main characteristic of the postmodern era we are living through. The previous phase of human development, which sociologists dub 'the modern era', was confident that purposive rationality would replace religious irrationality as the main guide for the human community, but that confidence has largely evaporated. As I shall try to show in the next movement, the main characteristic of the post-modern era is its lack of a single unifying story. Even Christians can't agree among themselves about the meaning and authority of the story they have been telling the world for 2,000 years. And while secular society gazes upon the endless feuds and disagreements of religion with lofty contempt, it has not been particularly good at supplying humanity with usable alternatives to the old, old story. There's a verse in the Book of Judges that captures the essence of the post-modern atmosphere, which suggests that it may not, after all, be such a new problem: 'In those days there was no king in Israel, but every man did that which was right in his own eyes.'[20] We seem to be inhabiting a cultural supermarket in which consumer choice is the only agreed value. One of the more intriguingly depressing side-effects of the present-day scene is that it has taken a lot of the pleasure out of dissonance and transgression. If everything is permitted, then nothing is much fun any longer. As the serpent knew well, if you want to get humans really interested in something, then erect a large sign prohibiting it. So, we might offer a post-modern revision of Dostoevsky's despairing cry: 'God, if everything is permitted, then where's the fun in anything?'

Now it's up to us

Before trying to find a positive way out of the predicament I have described, let me recall some of the tensions within both the stories I have outlined. The main tension in the Christian story lay in the split it established in human experience, especially between the divine command of perfection and the unavoidable human experience of failure. Within

Christianity this has produced enormous anxiety about the self. An American psychiatrist told me that he thanked God daily for the Church because it kept him lucratively in business. The main tension in today's scientific story comes from the sense that though we still need to restrain our tendency to chaos, the traditional way of grounding the moral life has lost its authority because it was part of an explanatory narrative that no longer compels our assent. This, too, produces enormous anxiety about self and society. We seem to be caught between a rock and a hard place, between opting back into the authoritarian children's home from which we have only recently escaped and finding ourselves wandering aimlessly in the atomised confusion that is today's society.

Before attempting a dramatic cliff-top rescue for endangered humanity, let me offer a few comments on some of the responses to the current situation we get from traditional religious leaders as well as from the columnists in the more conservative newspapers. There is no doubt that there has been a profound alteration in moral behaviour in society in the last forty years, but we should be wary of rushing too quickly to condemn it out of hand. Moral change has been a constant in human history, though it has recently accelerated in a most unsettling way. But there are gains as well as losses to report. If there has been a shift in European society away from the suppression of the pleasure principle to its undisciplined expression in private life, there have also been significant moral gains in the public sphere. Private individuals may be more self-indulgent and hedonistic today, but society and its systems are less cruel than they once were. That seems to me to be a worthwhile trade-off. In Britain we no longer send children down mines or up chimneys; we no longer execute criminals; we no longer send men to prison for loving members of their own sex; we no longer subject women to lifelong bondage in loveless and brutal marriages with no allowable legal exit for them. I could add almost indefinitely to that list. Of course, many point to major deficits in today's community ledger, mainly in the precariousness that now characterises stable sexual relationships, though this may only represent a more honest description of the reality of what has never actually been a simple picture. It is also worth pointing out that conservative social critics usually emphasise the weakening effect of liberal attitudes on humans today and do not pay enough attention to the revolutionary effects of the globalisation of the market economy on traditional cultures and fragile communities. It is often the people who benefit most from globalised capital who are most critical of the disorientation of its victims.

But the exclusively religious critique of current confusions is probably the one with the least coherence. It is one thing to agree with the view that if people really did believe they were going to be eternally punished after death for their misdeeds in this life it would radically modify their behaviour; it is quite another thing to try to re-establish the threat of eternal punishment as a workable or even principled justification for the moral life today. It's a bit like arguing that because there were fewer fatalities on the roads when we relied on horse-drawn transport, we should prohibit cars and force people back on to horses. Once a paradigm has lost its plausibility you can't really get it back again, although there are always groups who choose to hold on to it long after it has faded from general use.

But the scientific critique of the traditional

Christian story is also often wide of the mark. One trenchant critic puts it this way:

> Why, we must wonder, would the shaper of the universe have frittered away thirteen billion years, turning out quadrillions of useless stars, before getting around to the one thing he really cared about, seeing to it that a minuscule minority of earthling vertebrates are washed clean of sin and guaranteed an eternal place in its company?[21]

That kind of satire is great fun, but it misses the point. It is true that many Christian apologists have tried to adapt the Christian story to the new scientific paradigm in a way that opens them to the kind of challenge expressed by Frederick Crews in that quotation. Why *did* God hang around so long messing with the universe before getting round to the only thing he was interested in, which was arranging our existence? It is embarrassing when theologians try to conflate the Christian story with the current scientific narrative; and it is a mistake, however understandable, when scientists try to disprove the Christian story as though it were just another set of outdated scientific claims. The scientific attack on Christianity is excusable, however, because fundamentalist groups insist on marketing Christianity as science rather than as myth. While we are all entitled to our own opinions, we are not entitled to our own facts, which is why scientists cannot avoid getting drawn into the quagmire of the science versus religion debate. Scientists insist that when things are discovered about the universe, such as the fact that the earth goes round the sun, they stay discovered. Are we to assume, therefore, that we are living through another one of Kuhn's scientific revolutions, with the old paradigm, Christianity, staging a last ditch resistance, whether adaptively, like liberals, or defiantly, like fundamentalists, before being finally defeated and leaving the field to contemporary scientific secularism? I think that is a false and unhelpful polarization, though it is one for which Christians have only themselves to blame. They should stop trying to market Christianity as a science that describes how God micro-manages the universe and acknowledge that it is a profound myth that can still teach us much about the archaeology of our own souls.

There is no doubt that there is a sense of spiritual crisis in Europe today, not only over how we are to

the earth, nor in the earth, but only us, a generation comforting ourselves with the notion that we
have come at an awkward time, that our innocent
fathers are all dead – as if innocence had ever been
– and our children busy and troubled, and we ourselves unfit, not yet ready, having each of us chosen
wrongly, made a false start, failed, yielded to impulse
and the tangled comfort of pleasures, and grown
exhausted, unable to seek the thread, weak and
involved. But there is no one but us, there never has
been.[24]

The world is all before us, with its promise and threat,
and we will make of it what we will. It is possible that
we will use our new-found freedom to live in a way
that will precipitate catastrophe, another great Fall. If
we do, we will only have ourselves to blame. Ready
or not, we have come of age and are now responsible for what we make of ourselves. The thought may
frighten us or it may exhilarate us. As the school gates
close behind us, and we walk away from the past, we
are going to have to learn to love one another for our
own sake. We have lost the protection of the old certainties, it's true, but it is also quite liberating to be
responsible for ourselves at last. And maybe we have

learnt some enduring lessons from the stories we were taught during our race's childhood. Maybe the central lesson, that we should try to care for one another, has stuck. Milton told us in his great poem of human loss that Adam and Eve, 'hand in hand with wandering steps and slow through Eden took their solitary way'. Tessimond makes the same point, though less grandly, in another of his poems. The fact that we are now on our own makes it all the more imperative that we learn to reach out to one another 'sometimes hand to hand':

This is not Love perhaps – Love that lays down
Its life, that many waters cannot quench, nor the
    floods drown –
But something written in lighter ink, said in a lower
    tone:
Something perhaps especially our own:
A need at times to be together and talk –
And then the finding we can walk
More firmly through dark narrow places
And meet more easily nightmare faces:
A need to reach out sometimes hand to hand –
And then find Earth less like an alien land:
A need for alliance to defeat

The whisperers at the corner of the street:
A need for inns on roads, islands in seas, halts for
    discoveries to be shared,
Maps checked and notes compared:
A need at times of each for each
Direct as the need of throat and tongue for speech.[25]

III
LISTENING

3
PLAYING IT BY EAR

And the Lord God said, Behold the man is become as one
of us, to know good and evil... Therefore the Lord God sent
him forth from the garden of Eden . . . So he drove out the
man.

GENESIS

If we are on our own now because we have left the
shelter and security of one of the great religious
traditions, how are we to think about the complex
subject of morality? More importantly, how are we to
direct our lives now that we have left behind the
ordered systems that religion once provided? A good
place to begin is with the word 'morality' itself.
Morality has been unnecessarily mystified, mainly
because it has been associated with the supernatural
claims of the different religious traditions. Moses,
according to the Hebrew scriptures, received the Ten
Commandments directly from God in a ceremony
accompanied by the kind of impressive stage effects

that only God could provide. This gave to the moral life of the Israelites the support and authority of God himself. God's initiating role served to internalise and intensify the importance of the moral code and give great solemnity and power to its observance. But the variety of moral codes promoted by religion should alert us to the fact that there has always been something incurably plural and complex about the way communities have ordered their customs. The word 'morality' is derived from the Latin *mos*, and its genitive case *moris*, meaning a 'way', 'habit', 'manner' or 'fashion'. A moral system is the way a particular community chooses to organise its personal and group relations. The history of travel is replete with examples of the confusion that the variety of moral traditions can create for the unwary. Diderot provides an interesting example in his *Encyclopédie* under the heading 'enjoyment' (*jouissance*). He describes the visit of the ship *Bougainville* to Tahiti. The almoner of the ship was billeted with Orou. At bedtime Orou presented his wife and three daughters before the almoner and invited him to choose one as his companion for the night. The almoner replied that his religion, his office, good morals and decency would not allow him to accept the offer. To this Orou replied:

> I do not know what this thing is that you call 'religion'; but I can only think ill of it, since it prevents you from tasting an innocent pleasure to which nature, the sovereign mistress, invites us all; prevents you from giving existence to one of your own kind, from doing a service which a father, mother and children all ask of you, from doing something for a host who has received you well, and from enriching a nation by giving it one more citizen. I do not know what this thing is which you call your 'office', but your first duty is to be a man and to be grateful. I do not suggest that you should introduce into your country the ways of Orou, but Orou, your host and friend, begs you to lend yourself to the ways of Tahiti.'[1]

The modern reader is unlikely to approve of a code that permitted Orou to use his wife and daughters in this way. It lends support to the idea, which has been prevalent in history, that women are essentially the sexual property of men to be disposed of as they pleased. But the incident probably tells us more about the Tahitian hospitality code than about its sexual ethics. A more troubling example of the importance of ancient hospitality codes is found in a mysterious story in Genesis. We are told that two angels come to stay with Lot in Sodom. At bedtime the men of Sodom surround the house and demand that Lot let them have his guests for sex:

> And they called unto Lot, and said unto him, Where are the men which came in to thee this night? Bring them out unto us, that we may know them.

For Lot to comply with such a request would be a gross breach of the rules of hospitality. Instead, he offers them his daughters:

> Behold now, I have two daughters which have not known man; let me, I pray you, bring them out unto you, and do ye to them as is good in your eyes: only unto these men do nothing; for therefore came they under the shadow of my roof.[2]

Though it may seem bizarre to us for a father to volunteer his daughters for a gang-bang, it was less ethically disturbing to Lot than to breach the hospitality code by failing to protect his guests. A grosser example of the same phenomenon is found in the Book of Judges, chapter 19, which tells the story of a Levite who was travelling to Bethlehem to bring home his wife. He is invited by an old man to spend the night at his home. The story continues:

> Now as they were making their hearts merry, behold, the men of the city, certain sons of Belial, beset the house round about, and beat at the door, and spake to the master of the house, the old man, saying, Bring forth the man that came into thine house, that we may know him. And the man, the master of the house, went out unto them, and said unto them, Nay brethren, nay, I pray you, do not so wickedly; seeing that this man is come into my house, do not this folly. Behold, here is my daughter a maiden, and his concubine; them I will bring out now, and humble ye them, and do with them what seemeth good unto you; but unto this man do not so vile a thing. But the men would not hearken to him: so the man took his concubine, and brought her forth unto them; and they knew her, and abused her all the night until the morning: and when the day began to spring, they let her go. Then came the woman in the dawning of the day and fell down at the door of the man's house where her lord was, until it was light.

The distance between modern perceptions and these ancient codes is vast, but it should persuade us of the variety and elasticity of moral customs down the centuries.

The modern secular person is no longer confidently established at the heart of any of these codes and traditions in the way our ancestors were. There are a number of ways of describing the atmosphere of Western society at the beginning of the third millennium, but the one that is the easiest to understand is to think of our society as being at the end of tradition: ours is described as a post-traditional community, in the sense that no single tradition is in dominant control of human culture. It is true, of course, that there are still many strong religious traditions available, and they attract considerable loyalty from their adherents. But it is the variety on offer that is the key to the current scene. A tradition is a system of ideas and practices based on a set of assumptions from which a complex social or religious structure has evolved. Scholars sometimes call these underground streams of value and meaning 'metanarratives'. They inform us that since religious systems have lost their automatic authority over the lives of most people in our culture, Western society now lacks a strong sense of agreement on how to understand and order the life of human communities.

The end of tradition

This is a highly complex phenomenon, but it seems to have been produced by a number of factors, in addition to the straightforward erosion of religious authority by the constant surge of human knowledge, particularly in the sciences. One important factor is the way modern communications technology has shrunk the world. The jargon word here is *globalisation*. We are familiar with the idea of the world as a global village with a unified economic system, but it is a mistake to limit this metaphor to the economic system. Globalisation has profoundly affected the religious and intellectual currencies of the world as well as its economic systems. We are now keenly aware of the existence and power of other religions and traditions. Today we are so used to acknowledging the claims of different human cultures that we easily forget how new it is, particularly in the parts of the world that have been strongly influenced by the exclusivist claims of Christianity. Exclusivist traditions operate at their best when people are unaware that they are in one. Their tradition is not an arbitrary human construct, the way *they* happen to do things: it is the right way, the way things ought to be done, because it was ordained by God. This is why, for instance, when European colonists encountered the cultures of the native communities of the lands they invaded, they dismissed them as primitive and without value, rather in the way the almoner of the Bougainville responded to the hospitality of his host Orou. This cultural arrogance was the prelude to the destruction of ancient societies that often characterised European imperialism and the Christian expansionism that accompanied it.

There were always exceptions to this melancholy rule, of course. The history of Britain's encounter with Indian and Arab culture, for instance, provides examples of colonisers who so admired the traditions of the country they had been sent to conquer that they 'went native' and adopted its customs, including its religion, usually to the fury of more conventional imperialists. The irony is that today, in our spiritual confusion in the West, many people are turning back to certain aspects of the cultures our forebears held in contempt because they contain great wisdom, not least in their attitude to the earth and their reverence for creation.

Globalisation now makes it impossible for us to be unaware of other traditions, and other ways of looking at the world. The resulting shift in attitude is what we call pluralism. Indeed, *plural society* rather than *post-traditional society* might be a more accurate description of the kind of community we live in today. Ours is a multi-traditional society, but the very experience of encountering other cultures has an inevitably eroding effect on the way any single tradition is held. The term that is used to describe this process of cultural erosion is *relativism*, and there are two subtly different meanings to the term. One is descriptive: as a matter of fact, it says, your cultural tradition is relative to your social context and its inherited perspectives. If you were born in Ireland the chances are that you'll be a Catholic; if you were born in Turkey the chances are that you'll be a Muslim; if you were born in India the chances are that you'll be a Hindu. A better term for this process might be *perspectivalism*, to distinguish it from another meaning of relativism, which is the view that there is no way in which we can say that one kind of conduct is better than any other. Shortly, I shall challenge that view, but for the moment I simply want to establish that one of the inescapable aspects of our post-traditional society is that it generates an awareness that there are many cultures and value systems among human beings. That recognition inevitably complicates matters when we come to make moral judgements. Many people find that living in this kind of plural society induces confusion and anxiety in them. All the landmarks that once guided them have been moved around, so it is not surprising that some people feel lost and angry.

Fundamentalism

Before suggesting a way in which we might pick our way through the ethical complexities that face us in today's environment, I want to look briefly at two very different responses to the situation we are in. One fascinating response is what we might describe as defiant immobilism, a perspective that is loosely labelled 'fundamentalism'. Strictly speaking, fundamentalism is a late-nineteenth-century American Protestant response to the evolutionary theories that were beginning to erode traditional ways of understanding the Bible. Fundamentalists responded by simply asserting the verbal inerrancy of scripture. In Islam the position is more complex. While fundamentalists make up a sectarian element within Christianity, it could be argued that Islam by definition is intrinsically fundamentalist because it holds that in the Koran God has given a perfect revelation of the ideal society. This is why in the dominant Sunni branch of Islam it is claimed that 'the gates of interpretation' were closed around the year 900, ruling out any theoretical evolution in their religion.[3] However we account for its emergence in different religions, the psychology of this response to change is as straightforward as it is understandable. In a world of constant change and chance, clinging to the past is an obvious refuge. As Hilaire Belloc put it, it is a desperate holding on to nurse for fear of finding something worse. When we try to engage in conversation with religious immobilists we soon discover that no real converse is possible. They defiantly hold on to the tradition that is being threatened by new developments because they refuse to acknowledge the validity of any point of view other than the one into which they have been initiated. The paradox of this attitude is that its intransigence and refusal to negotiate new ways of understanding old traditions places the traditions themselves in great jeopardy because it alienates those who may still be sympathetic to religion but cannot embrace it in a form that does violence to their current consciousness. Generous-minded people who might otherwise tolerate fundamentalism as yet another harmless human eccentricity are becoming increasingly aware that it can pose a danger to the health of the human community because of the way its certainties are attractive to rootless and emotionally damaged people for whom it provides a haven and a cause. At the moment the most extreme version of this is the recruitment of impressionable young people into extremist Islamic sects, but it is a phenomenon that is present throughout the history of most religions. It is one of the most dangerously volatile elements in the world today, ranging from the wilder extremes of Christian fundamentalists in the USA and the ultra-Orthodox in Israel, right across to the restless and resentful turbulence of parts of the Muslim world.

Scepticism

If refusal to abandon ancient norms is an obvious and understandable response to the confusions of our era, its polar opposite is absolute moral relativism. This is a kind of extreme ethical scepticism which holds that once you abandon the directive power of religion there is no longer any basis on which you can promote authoritative moral choices. This is the point of view that was expressed by Bruno in Michel Houellbecq's novel *Atomised*. If you take this line, the work of the intellect becomes purely descriptive, informing us about how people behave in all their variety, but providing us with no basis for judging between them. One version of this is cultural relativism, which holds that no society has any grounds on which it can judge any other. So people outside India have no right to comment on that country's caste system, for instance; and people outside Africa have no right to comment on the practice of female circumcision.

But to admit that values conflict is not the same as saying that there are no values at all, no fundamental principles that can be said to characterise us as human. Apart from the few people in any society who seem to be completely lacking in love for their fellow humans, most of us would recognise some bond or similarity between ourselves and others. Aristotle bases his ethics on this instinctive sympathy humans have for each other: 'One may observe in one's travels in distant countries the feelings of recognition and affiliation that link every human being to every other human being.'[4] This is why the golden rule, which the old wife of Auchtermuchty recommended, advises us to do to others as we would have them do to us; or, to put it negatively, not to do to others what we would not want them to do to us. It is found in Matthew's Gospel chapter 7: 'All things whatsoever ye would that men should do to you, do ye even so to them.' It is also found in the sayings of Hillel, an influential Jewish teacher of the time of Jesus, so it was almost certainly used at the time as an encapsulation of the moral code. Using the golden rule as a general principle, you could map out a sensible ethic without any religious underpinning that would include most of the big items found in any of the traditional systems, such as: prohibitions against murder and violent assault; agreed ways of managing the complexities of human sexual relations, and mutual pacts against stealing and bearing false witness. A moment's thought will show that any human community that wanted to achieve a basic level of peace and harmony would be bound to establish some version of these fundamental requirements. We are all of us struggling to achieve some sort of personal happiness, and life is difficult enough without having others constantly invading and violating our personal space. Indeed, the instinct to protect our own physical and emotional territory is deeply implanted in us and is the source of the outrage we feel when it is violated by indifferent intruders.

Antonio Damasio has important things to say about understanding how these ancient instincts still drive our social relations:

> Understanding the biology of emotions, and the fact that the value of each emotion differs so much in our current human environment, offers considerable opportunities for understanding human behaviour.

We can learn, for example, that some emotions are terrible advisors and consider how we can either suppress them or reduce the consequences of their advice. I am thinking, for example, that reactions that lead to racial and cultural prejudices are based in part on the automatic deployment of social emotions evolutionarily meant to detect *difference* in others because difference may signal risk or danger, and promote withdrawal or aggression. That sort of reaction probably achieved useful goals in a tribal society but is no longer useful, let alone appropriate, to ours. We can be wise to the fact that our brain still carries the machinery to react in the way it did in a very different context ages ago. And we can learn to disregard such reactions and persuade others to do the same.[5]

One important side of the moral life, therefore, is the ability to understand and modify impulses that might have had survival value in a previous social context, but are counter-productive in the very different circumstances in which we now live. Freud said that civilisation is the price we pay to protect ourselves from nature, and he was talking about human nature in its undisciplined state. The moral life of a community is one of the ways it organises itself in order to survive and flourish. We may have abandoned a literal understanding of the religious myths that once gave supernatural authority to the systems we developed to protect ourselves from ourselves, but that does not mean that we can safely jettison the values we then fashioned. No matter what absolute moral relativists say, most people recognise the basic sanity of a system that allows them to live their lives in safety. However, the moral debates that obsess us are rarely about such basic issues, for the perfectly obvious reason that we take them for granted. There are few people against whom we have to defend our theoretical right not to be murdered in bed at night by armed robbers; but there are many who are likely to dispute with us the appropriate way to manage the challenges presented by the new genetic technologies. Finding our way round moral dilemmas that were not even thinkable five years ago is difficult enough; it is made more difficult when people are unaware of the massive assumptions on which they base their judgements. Once again, some of us get caught in the crossfire between competing extremes: between those who say that the law has already been laid down on everything and we have only to apply it, and those who say that there is now no basis on which we can make general moral judgements, so it's each man for himself.

How are we to respond to this polarisation between those who believe that tradition presents us with a fixed text, a single authoritative script that we must play from at all seasons and in all circumstances, and those who say that humanity is now hopelessly and permanently atomised into irreconcilable interest groups with no common ground on which to build an ethical society? Is the choice between playing the old hymn sheet over and over again or slipping into the chaos of the company of anarchic instrumentalists who insist on doing their own thing? To develop a metaphor I used in *Godless Morality*, I'd like to suggest improvisational jazz as a way of responding to the situation we face.[6] The best description of the essence of jazz I have come across is in Bill Evans' note to the Miles Davis album *Kind of Blue*. He describes a Japanese visual art form in which the artist is forced to be spontaneous. The pictures that result lack the complex composition and textures of classical painting,

but it is said that those who see will find something
, captured that escapes explanation. This conviction
that direct deed is the most meaningful reflection, I
believe, has prompted the evolution of the extremely severe and unique disciplines of the jazz or impro-
vising musician.[7]

Improvisation requires a high level of musicianship
from its practitioners – in our language, knowledge
of the moral tradition from which we come – but it
uses its skill and confidence to improvise, to depart
from the script or score, and create new music never
yet heard. Human genius has always done this. If it
hadn't, there would never have been new schools of
art or music or architecture; nor would there be
moral evolution and change in the way we understand and organise ourselves as human communities.
Evans says that Miles Davis arrived at the studio to
record what became one of the great jazz classics of
all time with a few sketches or settings. The group
had never played the pieces before the recording, so
what they produced was something close to pure
spontaneity.[8] Ethics is obviously a very different discipline to jazz, but it does have in common with it
the fact that it is a live performance in which its prac-

titioners have to respond to settings or situations which they may never have encountered before. Using the improvisational approach, I want to sketch five key settings that have to be dealt with by anyone who wants to contribute to moral reconstruction in our day:

- We expect to be asked
- We sometimes disagree
- We know that a sin is not a crime
- We confuse preferences with morality
- We are baffled by the ethics lag.

We expect to be asked

Traditional moral codes tended to emphasise the fundamental importance of obedience to the commandments of superior authority. This was understandable and appropriate in hierarchical cultures, when society was a social pyramid with God at the top, from whom all authority descended, through emperors and popes and barons and bishops and school masters and local doctors and policemen on the beat down to the lowliest subject. Everyone knew their place; everyone, except God, had to obey someone else. The whole thing worked beautifully and there was perfect social harmony, according to those who look back nostalgically to the traditional way of ordering society. We know, of course, that it was not all that wonderful, particularly if you were near the bottom of the pyramid; but the important thing for us to notice is that, whether we like it or not, there has been a social revolution that has swept most of that old order away. Today we expect to be listened to and our consent gained in areas that importantly affect our lives, because we refuse to be ordered around by those in power, even if they think they are doing it for our own good. Here's an example from a few years ago to illustrate the point.

It was a scandal that began almost absent-mindedly, with a throwaway remark that started a nightmare. A witness at the Bristol Babies Heart Surgery Inquiry revealed that the Royal Liverpool Children's Hospital had one of the biggest and best collections of children's hearts in Britain. That was the beginning of the organs retention scandal that outraged British public opinion and seriously damaged the reputation of the UK medical community. It turned out that more than

100,000 hearts, lungs, brains and other organs were being held by hospitals in the UK, and many of these organs had been taken from patients whose relatives had no idea that they had buried incomplete corpses. The most sickening detail in the grim landscape that was gradually revealed was the head of an eleven-year-old boy found at one hospital. At the Scottish end of the story, Professor Sheila McLean's report revealed that more than 5,000 human body parts, of which at least 1,000 were from children, were stored in hospitals across the country, some from as long ago as 1953.

Behind the humiliation and bewilderment that characterised the response of the medical profession to the scandal there lay a complex tangle of good intentions and old-fashioned paternalism. During the inquiries into the stolen organs, outraged families said again and again, 'If only they had asked.' But, in the days when these organs were being harvested at the behest of the doctors, not enough asking was done by any profession in any area of life. Bernard Shaw said that every profession was a conspiracy against the laity, and it is easy to see why. In complex societies, people learn to specialise in particular subjects and then sell their expertise to the ignorant lay person. Even though most people are well-intentioned, there is something about power that invariably corrupts the human imagination. And knowledge is power. Anyone in possession of knowledge that is important for me, but of which I myself am ignorant, has enormous power over me. The natural assumption that good-hearted but unimaginative people in authority make is that since their purposes are benign, any methods they use to achieve them ought to be excused. The good end justifies the thoughtless arrogance of the means.

Outrage over the organ retention scandal served to puncture that kind of paternalism. It led to greater rigour in the use of consent procedures, but the most significant thing about it is that it showed that a dramatic culture shift had already taken place in Britain: the age of paternalism was over, the age of accountability had arrived. Like everything human, the new culture of accountability is flawed and has already manufactured unintended problems, mainly because of the increase in paperwork and bureaucracy that is a necessary accompaniment of the new consent procedures. That is why it is important to recognise that social evolution is not necessarily the same thing as human progress, in the sense that things necessarily get better as we leave the battered old ways behind. As a matter of fact, I think that many aspects of post-traditional culture are a considerable improvement on the way things were done previously, but, as we have already noted, there have been losses as well as gains. The new thing that has emerged is a mistrust of the old, secret, authoritarian way of running things and a demand for greater transparency. However, this dramatic shift in the way we want society to be run today should demonstrate to us how fragile and pro-visional social traditions are. We should hold them firmly enough to make them operate efficiently, but not so tightly that we are unable to recognise the moment when a major change of direction is com-ing and go with it. One of the things we have to listen out for is the future itself, because it has a habit of creeping up on us so softly that we don't see it coming.

Human sexuality
Another area in which the new culture of listening and consenting has important effects is in the area of

human sexuality. The old authoritarian traditions, particularly in their Christian form, had a highly functional, but essentially disapproving, attitude to sex: it was grudgingly permitted for the purposes of procreation, though even here its use was severely circumscribed. This led to a system that operated like a licensing authority which issued performance certificates to qualified practitioners. Since the purpose of sex was procreation, any form of licensed sex that was not 'open' to conception, as the official phrase put it, was condemned. Notoriously, this ruled out any kind of sexual activity between members of the same sex, and any kind of sexual activity that used barriers against conception. As with any system of prohibition, this had the effect of making sex even more fascinating to us. Nietzsche described the resulting complex in these words:

> *To think a thing evil means to make it evil.* – The passions become evil and malicious if they are regarded as evil and malicious. Thus Christianity has succeeded in transforming Eros and Aphrodite into diabolical phantoms by means of the torments it introduces into the consciences of believers whenever they are excited sexually. Is it not dreadful to make necessary

and recurring sensations into a source of inner misery, and in this way to want to make inner misery a
necessary and regularly recurring phenomenon *in
every human being*! In addition to which it remains a
misery kept secret and thus more deeply rooted.
Must everything that one has to combat, that one has
to keep within bounds or on occasion banish totally
from one's mind, always have to be called evil! The
sexual sensations have this in common with the sensations of sympathy and worship, that one person, by
doing what pleases him, gives pleasure to another
person – such benevolent arrangements are not to
be found so very often in nature![9]

In this passage, Nietzsche is careful to point out that
the sexual instinct may on occasion have to be com-
bated, kept within bounds, or even banished from
one's mind. This is because sex is a powerful force, and
powerful forces always have to be handled with care,
the way we might handle a spirited horse; but that is
far from identifying sex as evil or wrong in itself. It is
the demonising of sex in Christianity that is at the
root of some of its most vexing problems, such as its
struggle to come to terms with the fact of gay sexuality. Most of the early theologians were physically
squeamish about sex. They did not like the thought

Going to war

Another interesting development in current ethical theory is the application of the principle of informed consent to war. Declaring war is one of the most jealously guarded powers of government, but there are signs that this is being challenged. The classic approach to the ethics of war is the theory of the Just War, a doctrine which was developed over a thousand years ago. It says that for a war to be justified it must satisfy five criteria: (a) the cause must be just; (b) it has to be declared by legitimate authority; (c) there has to be probability of success; (d) there has to be proportionality in the means, and (e) there has to be non-combatant immunity. These criteria were measurable, at least in theory, when wars were fought between armies using conventional weapons on battle-fields far from centres of population. It is the final two criteria that raise the strongest moral challenge today: proportionality in the means and immunity for non-combatants. Many thinkers believe that there can be no ethical justification for modern warfare today, because the means used are now more damaging to civilians than to the soldiers themselves. The military doctrine of the USA is the best example of this development. To minimise casualties among its troops, America applies massive force in its military adventures abroad, as well as in its policing methods at home. Using sophisticated high-tech weapons from a distance, it pulverises areas that may contain enemy soldiers, with devastating consequences for any civilians in the vicinity, whose deaths it describes as 'collateral damage'. In modern scientific warfare there is no such thing as non-combatant immunity. Bombs dropped from a mile up in the sky don't discriminate between soldiers and civilians. This is why the world is littered with vast refugee settlements as large as cities and awash with uprooted peoples, all displaced by the hurricane of modern conflict.

It has always been more difficult for leaders of liberal democracies to get their people to go to war than for leaders in authoritarian or despotic societies. This is particularly the case in democracies today, where their populations are highly educated, which is why a sixth principle, consent by the people, is being tacitly added to the Just War theory. The Second Iraq War, in 2003, was a good illustration both of this theory in practice and of how easily it can be manipulated by political leaders. There was little appetite in Britain for this war. I do not intend to rehearse the arguments surrounding the event because little new can be said about them. But I do want to reflect briefly on the way the British government gained the consent of its people to allow the conflict to proceed. Most people have an instinctive revulsion against war, but they share an equally instinctive sense that it is right for people to protect themselves against the aggressions of others. History generates monstrous people against whom we must defend ourselves. That is why most of us believe, however reluctantly, in the appropriateness of using force as a last resort in defending ourselves against naked and dangerous aggression. This, presumably, was why the Prime Minister of Great Britain and the President of the USA sought to persuade their populations not just that Saddam Hussain was a monstrous tyrant but that he was also an imminent danger to them. Because of the continuing trauma of the American people after 9/11, the task of gaining the consent of the people to the adventure was easier in the USA than it was in Britain. The British Prime Minister did manage to persuade a majority of the British population that the Iraqi dictator was an imminent danger to them. The fact that, in hindsight, his arguments are now deemed to have been fraudulent, and that the war was entered not to protect Britain, but to effect regime change in Iraq, does not undermine the principle of informed consent to wars by the people whose taxes pay for them and whose children have to fight them. My hunch is that the practice of gaining consent by the people to foreign wars will become increasingly important in Britain. And I am convinced that if Britain ever engages in another foreign aggression the reasons in support of it will have to be more manifest and transparent than the ones given in March 2003.

We sometimes disagree

One of the most difficult things for us to learn is that good moral systems can be in conflict. A tragic illustration of this principle was the case of the conjoined twins who were brought to Britain from Malta in 2000. In Britain the law allows adults to refuse medical treatment if it goes against their religious or moral principles. So, for instance, the adult follower of a religion that prohibits blood transfusion can refuse such treatment, even if it is the only thing that would save his or her life. But the law does not allow adults to make these life-or-death decisions on behalf of their children. When the doctors examined Mary and Jodie, the conjoined twins in question, they discovered that Mary was parasitic on Jodie. They immediately realised that both would die if they were not separated, but that Jodie's life could be saved if they intervened. When the parents refused to consent to the operation, the doctors went to court to override their opposition. The debate that ensued throughout Britain showed just how mature and careful we can be when we discuss complex moral issues. Each side was respectful of the other, though the moral divide between them was profound. Dame Mary Warnock, the doyenne of British ethicists, made the case for separating the twins. Using a traditional argument called 'the law of double effect', she said that in separating the twins the moral intention was to save the life of Jodie, though the tragic secondary or double effect of that primary intention would be the death of Mary. Since the intention was to save the life of Jodie, Mary's death would not be murder, it would be the tragic but unintended consequence of rescuing her sister. Without that intervention, neither sister would live and the opportunity to save one of them would be lost. The other point of view was argued, with equal cogency, by the Roman Catholic Archbishop of Westminster, who said that it was never morally right to kill one innocent person in order to save the life of another. Even though the primary intention might be to save Jodie, the fact that it was known that Mary would die in the process made her death an inescapable and intended part of the operation. The judge ruled on the side of separation, the procedure went ahead, and Mary subsequently died. It is comforting to report that Jodie is today a happy little girl, whose parents are now glad the operation took place.

That debate highlighted a principle we should acknowledge when we discuss morality: good people can disagree with each other for valid reasons, and good moral traditions can be in tragic conflict. In fact, few of our disputes are between an obvious good and an obvious evil; more frequently they are between opposing goods. In the case of the conjoined twins, we saw two good moral traditions at work, reaching different conclusions, though a choice between them had to be made. The lesson we should learn from this is that respect for opposing points of view is itself an important moral principle, particularly in our increasingly plural society. Just because you feel passionately about something does not give you the right to dismiss your opponent as immoral. Of course, your opponent may be in the grip of irrational fears, but it is just as likely that she is operating from a different value system to yours. Though her morals may be different from yours, they are *morals*, not evidence of corruption. Once again, we see the importance of listening hard, this time to those with whom we may profoundly disagree.

We know that a sin is not a crime

The next thing to note is that there is a difference between sin and crime. Because religious groups themselves do not always grasp this distinction, they often add more heat than light to moral debate in today's society. If you belong to a religious group, then certain activities may be forbidden to you because they are believed to be sinful, such as eating certain kinds of food or indulging in certain kinds of sexual activity or undergoing certain kinds of surgical procedure. In free societies, religious groups have a right to require these disciplines of their followers; they have no right to try to impose them on society at large through the legislative system. This fact creates a double burden: religious people have to live with the fact that the state may permit activities they deem to be sinful; but secular people have to acknowledge that religious freedom is an important value in their society, including the right to hold unfashionable views. Again, we move inevitably to the importance of tolerance in a culture where different value systems are in constant conflict.

Abortion is probably the keenest version of this particular debate, with those who are passionately motivated to defend what they call the rights of 'the unborn' engaged in a permanent campaign to over-turn a piece of legislation that most people favour. The issue of abortion is another example of the tragic choices that often characterise the moral life. In this case it is the tension between the potential life of the unborn child and the actual life of the mother. When abortion is made illegal it does not cease, it just moves into the underworld of back-street abortionists and do-it-yourself kits for desperate women, where it causes misery and death. This is why, in addition to all the other shades of opinion expressed in the abortion debate, it is possible to be anti-abortion and pro-choice at the same time. It is also why many people promote the use of improved birth control techniques, particularly the morning-after pill. The practical solution to the abortion epidemic is better sex education and freely available and intelligently used contraception.

It is hard for members of traditional moral communities to coexist with people in society who differ radically from them in important ways; but the secular community has to cope with the difficulty of living in a society that exempts religious communities from the European Equal Treatment directive, which bans discrimination at work on the grounds of sexual orientation. A good example of the liberal tolerance that is extended to illiberal religious bodies comes from Canada, where the Ontario Court of Appeal recently ruled in favour of legalising marriages of same-sex couples. The Federal Government drafted legislation that changed the definition of marriage to 'the lawful union of two persons to the exclusion of all others'. But the legislation also went on to preserve the right of religious institutions 'to refuse to conduct marriage ceremonies that are not in accordance with their religious beliefs'. A similar proposal for the civil registration of same-sex partnerships is currently (2004) before the British Parliament. Unfortunately, some religious communities are incapable of the kind of tolerance that living in plural communities requires of them. The Roman Catholic Church recently called on Catholic politicians in democratic legislatures to oppose any move to permit the legal registration of same-sex partnerships. This is a fateful and tragic development. The Catholic Church has the right to command its members to desist from practices it deems to be sinful; it has no right to order elected politicians in secular democracies to legislate on purely confessional grounds. The Vatican's unfortunate intervention is likely to have two regrettable if unintended consequences. Voters will get into the dangerous habit of interrogating the religious beliefs of politicians running for election, a development which could lead to an unhappy reversion to sectarian prejudice. Just as likely is the possibility that secular politicians, who resent bullying tactics, will call for the removal of the exemptions that permit religious institutions to abrogate some of

the most significant human rights protections in the
European Community.

We confuse preferences with morality

Another important and related distinction that's
worth noting is the difference between a moral
judgement and a personal preference. For example,
you may be revolted at the mere thought of sexual
intimacy between persons of the same sex, but if you
can't clearly show who is harmed by it, as opposed
to insistently stating that it should be forbidden
because you disapprove of it, then the chances are
that you are expressing a personal preference or a
religious conviction, not a moral judgement. A
good working definition of a wrong act is one that
'manifestly harms others or their interests, or violates
their rights or causes injustice'. Human nature is
enormously varied and eccentric, so we have to be
careful not to elevate our own preferences and
convictions to the status of absolute moral law. It is
important in a healthy society to establish the difference between legitimate human diversity and conduct that is injurious to others. That is why one of

the most profound questions we have to ask ourselves is about the legitimate role of the state in policing private behaviour. The great conservative political philosopher Edmund Burke had interesting things to say on this subject:

> It is better to cherish virtue and humanity by leav-ing much to free will, even with some loss to the object, than to attempt to make men mere machines and instruments of a political benevolence. The world on the whole will gain by a liberty without which virtue cannot exist.[11]

Remembering our definition of a morally wrong act as something that manifestly harms others, it is obvious that the state has a duty to protect me from the unwelcome attentions of others; it is not so easy to define its duty to protect me from myself. Given the ugly history of state interference in the lives of private individuals, we should be extremely cautious in this area. For centuries the state thought it had a right to discriminate against women, by denying them the right to vote or the right to divorce their husbands. We look back on those days with amazement, as we shall one day look back on the history of discrimination against

gay and lesbian people in Church and State. So it is a
sensible presumption not to intervene too promiscu-
ously in the private lives of people, unless we can clearly
demonstrate that their choices manifestly injure others
or violate their right to live in peace. Apart from anything else, laws that invade private space are invariably
flouted and bring the legal system itself into disrepute,
as is the case with the expensively unsuccessful war
against drugs both in Britain and in the US.
Government interference in the pleasures people pur-
sue to alleviate the strains of existence are invariably
mistaken and counter-productive. Most people need
methods of escape from time to time and most of them
manage their use of them with reasonable prudence,
though a tragic minority end up as permanent casualties. Freud said some interesting things on the subject:

> Life, as we find it, is too hard for us; it brings us too
> many pains, disappointments and impossible tasks. In
> order to bear it we cannot dispense with palliative
> measures. There are perhaps three such measures:
> powerful deflections, which cause us to make light of
> our misery; substitutive satisfactions, which diminish
> it; and intoxicating substances, which make us insen-
> sitive to it. Something of the kind is indispensable.[12]

Wise governments, like wise parents, will recognise the role these deflections play in our lives and will be cautious about intruding into such a complex area. Unfortunately, governments throughout history have clumsily interfered in the private choices of individuals, usually with devastating consequences. The war against drugs in Britain and the USA is probably the most devastating contemporary example of the havoc that such blundering interventions create. By prohibiting the use of a range of euphoric substances used by people to give themselves pleasure and ease the strains of life, these governments have not succeeded in eradicating the use of the drugs in question. But their clumsy interventions have had two devastating consequences: they have made criminals of millions of otherwise law-abiding citizens who refuse to consent to laws they passionately disagree with; and they have delivered the supply system for the banned substances into the hands of criminals who have become immensely wealthy as a result, and whose wealth has taken them beyond the reach of the law enforcement agencies. Politicians are beginning to speak out on the subject. One of them, Representative Tom Campbell from California, observed in 2000:

Look at our drugs war over the last 20 years and measure drug availability by the street price of heroin and cocaine. This price is one quarter of what it was 20 years ago. Since 1980 the number of drug overdose deaths has increased by 540%. The proportion of high school seniors reporting that drugs are readily available has doubled. Incarceration for drug offences has increased tenfold. The purity of heroin on the streets has increased more than four times. We've spent a quarter of a trillion dollars since 1980 . . . and this war on drugs is a failure.[13]

Governor Gary Johnson of New Mexico is another politician who is beginning to question the conventional wisdom:

There were 450,000 American deaths last year from tobacco, 150,000 from booze and 100,000 from legal prescription drugs. You know how many people died from marijuana? Well, I'm sure there were a few. You know how many died from heroin and cocaine? 5,000. Now where is the bogey man here?[14]

Comparable statistics could be provided from the British experience of the same policy. What seems to be missing from the analysis is any awareness of the arbitrariness of allowing government to choose from all the plants that grow on the earth which ones it will license for recreational use and which ones it will ban. It will allow me to smoke myself to death by the excessive use of the tobacco plant; but it refuses me the right to impair my mental processes by the excessive use of the marijuana plant. The argument against liberalising the law on drugs is that drugs damage our health. That is undoubtedly true, though it is worth repeating again and again that the most damaging of the recreational drugs are the legal ones. But the argument from the potential danger of these substances is one that can apply to almost anything we are inclined to use to excess. One of the big killers in Scotland is deep-fried fast food, but no government would dare ban fish suppers or close down McDonalds. What they sensibly try to do is educate people about healthier ways of eating. A wise operating maxim for government is that it is better to promote the good than to try to extirpate evil. Licensing the use of all recreational drugs, taxing them hard, and educating people about their dangers, would be the sanest policy for government, but it won't happen anytime soon, mainly because of the atmosphere of hysteria that surrounds the debate in Britain and the USA. Meanwhile we should encourage our politicians to read John Stuart Mill's essay *On Liberty*, particularly this celebrated passage:

> The only purpose for which power can be rightfully exercised over any member of a civilised community, against his will, is to prevent harm to others. His own good, either physical or moral, is not a sufficient warrant. He cannot rightfully be compelled to do or forebear because it will be better for him to do so, because it will make him happier, because, in the opinion of others, to do so would be wise or even right.[15]

We are baffled by the ethics lag

The acceleration of human knowledge always creates what we might describe as an 'ethics lag'. The history of morality is the story of how changing circumstances constantly outdistance the theories we created to guide us through earlier periods. The ethical conflict generated by the new genetics is the most eloquent example of this tension. Some years ago I took a geneticist friend out to lunch and asked him to tell me what he did all day in his laboratory. His particular branch of science was more mysterious to me than quantum physics or anything I had ever come across in theology. Patiently, he tried to tell me what DNA was. He explained that the body is made up of many different cells that perform different tasks. Genes instruct the cells on how they should operate. They provide the instructions for our development from a fertilised egg to a fully grown adult. Genes are sections of DNA (deoxyribonucleic acid) that are contained in the chromosomes that were passed on from our parents. Unfortunately, they are not infallible in the way they operate and terrible things can happen if they get the message wrong. When the human genome was completely mapped in 2001 we discovered that we have between 30,000 and 80,000 genes. We also know that there are as many as 5,000 known genetic disorders.[16] Approximately 2 per cent of all babies born each year have a genetic defect.

My friend was particularly committed to combating a terrible disease called cystic fibrosis, which affects the lungs and digestive system. In the lungs CF causes increasingly severe respiratory problems; in the

digestive tract it often results in extreme difficulty in
digesting adequate nutrients from food. Cystic fibrosis
occurs when a child inherits two copies of the defective CF gene, one from each parent. About 4 per cent
of the population may be carrying the defective gene,
though they themselves do not have the disease.
However, if both parents of a child are carriers there
is a 25 per cent chance with each pregnancy that the
child will be born with CF. My friend told me that
there was no known cure for CF, although methods
for managing the disease were becoming more
sophisticated. However, there was something that
could be done, but it carried a moral cost. Where both
parents were known to be carriers of the defective
gene, the woman could be screened to discover
whether the child she was carrying would be born
with the disease. The usual presumption behind the
screening test was that if the disease were detected in
the foetus the pregnancy would be terminated. I
remember thinking at the time that each advance in
human knowledge always seems to bring new moral
problems with it. My friend could provide a couple
with the information that their child was likely to be
born with a difficult and incurable disease, but he

could not help them in their struggle with the ethics of abortion.

In the 1990s, scientists discovered a possible new approach to the management of genetic diseases like cystic fibrosis. Reproductive technology is one of the fastest growing fields in applied science, but each development removes one moral problem only to install another. What is called pre-implantation genetic diagnosis provides carrier parents with another option in the management of their genetic condition. Instead of waiting for a pregnancy that might have to be terminated after screening, the couple could decide to use *in vitro* fertilisation (IVF) as a screening method. This would mean creating several embryos by the usual method of mixing sperm and eggs in a dish (IVF), then testing the embryos to see if they had the CF gene. Only embryos free of the defective gene would be put back in the mother. Here science has eased the moral problem of abortion but, for some people, it has created a new difficulty. According to some moral traditions, the embyro is an unborn human being with full moral rights. Most people would probably agree that discarding microscopic embryos is less morally disturbing than aborting a fourteen-week foetus, so they would probably welcome the advent of pre-implantation genetic diagnosis as an improvement on the old technology of screening followed by termination. Until, that is, they read in the papers that in the US a profoundly deaf lesbian couple had used this technology to create a profoundly deaf baby. Most people would scratch their heads over the strangeness of using a technology designed to screen out genetic diseases in order to select a child bearing a specific defect, such as profound deafness. Building disability into a child is not what springs to mind when we think about designer babies, but the possibility does make us think. In the US there is little Federal control of these new reproductive technologies, but in Britain the Human Fertilisation and Embryology Authority regulates them, and it specifically prohibits this kind of practice.

The important thing to notice about all this is that the human passion for knowledge and discovery always has a downside. We create convenient new methods of transportation that shrink the world, but planes, trains and automobiles kill more than distance; they kill people as well. The Internet enables me to be instantly in touch with my daughter in the US, but it also facilitates the activities of international paedophile rings. Nothing scares us quite as much at the moment as the possibilities created by the new genetic technologies. Some commentators promise us a future of wealthy clones, with the bodies of film stars and the intellects of Nobel prize winners, who will hire women whose eggs they will harvest to clone embryos in order to farm them for spare parts. In this way, death will be endlessly postponed for a wealthy elite. An even more worrying possibility is that genetic engineering and biotechnology could transmogrify humanity's physique and mentality in the not too distant future if the technology enabling parents to 'design' genetically advantaged children were exploited by the wealthy. In his fascinating but pessimistic book *Our Final Century*, Martin Rees, the Astronomer Royal, quotes Lee Silver's book *Remaking Eden* as saying it would only take a few generations for humanity to divide into two species, what he calls the 'GenRich' and the 'Naturals'.[17] Given the over-heated atmosphere that surrounds the promise and threat of the new genetic technologies, it is worth reminding ourselves that we always tend to panic when the pace of human discovery speeds up. Part of what is going on is the usual resistance of the average human to change, and the pain of having to get our minds round new ways of thinking and operating. But there is no doubt that the science of genetics has added a new fear to our repertoire of anxiety. This is the very stuff of life we are meddling with, and something inside us feels that it would be better if it were all left to nature or chance or god. We admire scientists, but we worry about the way they sometimes allow themselves to be seduced into doing terrible things. So we feel that scientists should not be left to establish the ends to which their discoveries are put. And our natural anxieties can be amplified by the activities of special interest groups, who are often expert at opposing the onward march of science.

For example, how arc we to respond to those who claim that the embryo is an unborn person with full human rights? To claim that potentiality and actuality are the same thing, that because a group of cells, circumstances permitting, could develop into a full human being it must be endowed with the full panoply of human rights, is stretching things beyond sense. To accept that logic would make male masturbation tantamount to genocide, because semen also has the potential, circumstances permitting, to become a human being. Indeed, before the processes of human fertilisation were understood, it was believed that the male sperm was the carrier of a miniature human being, the homunculus, which was implanted in the woman's womb, where it was sheltered till it was big enough to be born. The legislators who crafted the Human Fertilisation and Embryology Act of 1990 believed that the human embryo had to be treated with reverence and respect, but they did not believe that it was an actual human being in miniature. The Act permits experiments on spare embryos to improve our understanding of human reproduction. The spare embryos can be used for only 14 days, when cell differentiation begins to take place. Pro-life groups have never liked the 1990 Act, but they have tried to make use of it for their own ends, as happened in the following case.

In 1997 Ian Wilmut and the team at the Roslin Institute near Edinburgh were trying to improve animal husbandry when they created Dolly, the first cloned animal. They were opposed to human reproductive cloning, and they sometimes even suggested that they were uncertain about whether animal cloning would ever be a really useful technology. With scientific development, it is often the by-product of a new technology that turns out to be the most useful to humanity. The exciting consequence of the work with cloning lies in its application to human scientific medicine. Dolly was cloned by transferring the nucleus of a body cell into an egg that had its own nucleus removed. Most mainstream scientists are opposed to using this technology to clone human beings, mainly because they cannot conceive of any ethical way to make the procedure safe, but they are strongly in favour of using it to create embryos that can be used in the treatment of genetic diseases. They make a distinction, in other words, between therapeutic cloning and reproductive cloning.

Medical scientists hope to be able to cure genetic disease by the use of stem cells from cloned embryos. Stem cells are the master cells found in early-stage embryos. They evolve into all the tissues of the body. By implanting and directing the development of these cells, doctors hope to be able to cure many conditions that are at present incurable, such as cystic fibrosis, diabetes and Parkinson's disease. Another advantage of this approach is that cells from the person with the disease could be used in the treatment, thereby overcoming the problem of rejection that complicates transplantation techniques at the moment. So the search for a cure for cystic fibrosis may soon be successful. What bedevils discussion of this promising medical technology is its association with the controversy over the cloning of actual human beings. The purpose of somatic cell nuclear transfer is to produce stem cells, not children. Why oppose it, then? Most people don't. While President Bush banned it in the US, the Government in Britain had wanted it to go ahead, but it nearly went badly wrong. It was thought that the 1990 Act would cover the new technique, thereby bringing it under regulatory control. But the Pro-Life Alliance almost capsized the whole regulatory framework. In 2001 they took the British Government to court in an attempt to prove that the 1990 Act did not cover the new biotechnology. They argued that in the Act the definition of an embryo was the fusion of sperm and egg, whereas the new process involved nuclear transfer, so current legislation did not cover it. Perversely, had they succeeded in sabotaging the new technology they would have opened up Britain to the unregulated operations of eccentric scientists determined to clone human beings. A High Court decision agreed with the Pro-Life Alliance, but the judgment was later overturned on appeal in 2002, so in Britain we can now reap the medical benefits of this new technology.

The whole episode is morally instructive. It shows that in Britain there is an attempt to direct the new reproductive technologies in a moderate and sensible way that will benefit the human community. We neither fall into a panic and ban every new scientific development that comes out of the lab, nor do we just leave scientists to get on with whatever they are up to without reference to the common good. We try to follow the path of appropriate regulation. The point I am trying to make in offering these examples, and the principles that flow from them, is that they all cause distress to particular groups who are disturbed by the variety of moral systems on offer in our plural society. Though most of the conflicts we engage in are between opposing goods, conflicting values, rather than between straight right and straight wrong, this does not mean that we can never make a decision and go for one of the options in a particular conflict. Managing these intractable disagreements in a plural culture is difficult. We have to accept the tragic fact that men and women are capable of making different choices on perfectly valid grounds, so considerable magnanimity will be required of us, if we are to live peaceably in plural moral communities.

Is there any ethical yardstick that we can use in evaluating these complex issues? One possible approach is found in one of the most influential books of social philosophy in the twentieth century. In *A Theory of Justice*,[18] John Rawls argued that if we were setting out with a blank sheet of paper to create a society founded upon principles chosen by rational citizens in what he called 'the original position', working behind a 'veil of ignorance' that prevented people from skewing their choices by their own abilities or place in society, we would choose a system that granted the most extensive liberties to its citizens while ensuring the maximum justice. In other words, if we did not know where we were going to be placed in the hypothetical society we were drawing up, we would be inclined to make it more fair and equal than most societies are today. Using Rawl's basis of 'the original position', we could argue that we should use the new technologies that flow from scientific research to help those whose lives are limited by disease and social deprivation, but that we should prevent the selfish exploitation of those technologies by those who would use them to enhance their already privileged status. The 'original position' provides us with a useful guiding principle that may help us to interrogate the unadmitted assumptions that we all bring to our analysis of society. Applying the principle of equal justice to the bewildering developments that constantly confront us means we'll have to pay close attention to what is going on. And like good jazz players, we might just learn that it is exhilarating to play life by ear.

IV
LEAVING

4

AFTER ALL

The leaves fall early this autumn, in wind . . .
They hurt me. I grow older.

EZRA POUND

We are always old enough to die. The young may find that hard to believe, but when you reach seventy, the life span allotted to us by the Bible,[1] it becomes increasingly obvious. Frequent attendance at the funerals of contemporaries concentrates the mind on the lateness of the hour and the shortness of the time that lies ahead. Of course, the mournful awareness that everything comes to an end is by no means the preserve of the elderly. Some of us have been mildly addicted to it all our lives. That's why I was pleased to read in Jan Morris' *Trieste and the Meaning of Nowhere* that Aristotle thought that all interesting people had a touch of melancholy in their make-up. It is her genius for melancholy that has always attracted me to Jan Morris, and it certainly suffuses what she has described as her final book. On the first page of the prologue she writes:

> There are moments in my life when a suggestion of Trieste is summoned so exactly into my consciousness that wherever I am I feel myself transported there. The sensation is rather like those arcane moments of hush that sometimes interrupt a perfectly ordinary conversation, and are said to signify the passing of an angel. Perhaps on biblical grounds – something to do with the Crucifixion? – these are popularly supposed to happen at ten minutes before the hour, and it is odd how frequently they do.

She describes herself as standing, in her imagination, on the waterfront of Trieste, and continues:

> None of my responses to these scenes are exuberant, but they are not despondent either. I am homesick, I am thinking sad thoughts about age, doubt and disillusion, but I am not unhappy. I feel there are good people around me, and an unspecified yearning steals narcotically over me – what the Welsh call *hiraeth*. Pathos is part of it, but in a lyrical form to which I

am sentimentally susceptible, and at the same time I am excited by a suggestion of sensual desire. The allure of lost consequence and faded power is seducing me, the passing of time, the passing of friends, the scrapping of great ships! The Trieste effect, I call it. It is as though I have been taken, for a brief sententious glimpse, out of time to nowhere.[2]

I am prone to these moments myself, though I associate them not with Trieste, but with long train journeys. There comes a moment, maybe at ten minutes before the hour, when businessmen stop shouting into their phones, a hush falls over the carriage, you put your novel down and look sadly out of the window. I had one of these moments not very long ago and the power of it has stayed with me since. I was reading John Banville's novel *The Untouchable* as I travelled from London to Edinburgh. As the train slowed to go through Newark Station I reached the place where Victor Maskell,[3] the central character, goes back to Carrickdrum to bury his father, a Church of Ireland bishop. But he has come to do more than bury his father and comfort Hettie, his stepmother. He has also come to place Freddie, his severely mentally handicapped brother, in a home. At first Freddie thinks they are going for a jaunt in the bishop's big old Daimler, and he gurgles with excitement. But when he is shown round the grim establishment where he is to spend what is left of his life he begins to panic:

> 'Come along now, Frankie,' the Sister was saying to Freddie, 'come along and we'll get you settled in.' He leaned toward her docilely, but then, as if he had bethought himself, he gave a violent start and shied away from her, goggling, and shaking his head, and making a choking noise at the back of his throat. He clutched at me, sinking his shockingly strong fingers into my arm. He had realised at last what was happening, that this was no treat laid on for him, a sort of pantomime, or an anarchic version of the circus, but that here was where he was to be abandoned, the bold corner where, for misdemeanours he could not recall committing, he was to be made to stand for the rest of his life.

But Hettie takes charge. She calms Freddie and leads him back upstairs to the bleak little room they have reserved for him, where she unpacks his bag. Banville continues:

> Freddie wandered about the room for a while, crooning to himself, then stopped at the bed and sat down, holding his back very straight, and with his knees together and his hands placed flat on the mattress at his sides. And then, having settled himself, the good boy once more, he lifted his eyes and looked at me where I stood cowering in the doorway, and smiled his most ingenuous, most beatific, smile, and seemed – surely I imagine it? – seemed to nod, once, as if to say, *Yes, yes, don't worry, I understand.*[4]

At that point my eyes misted over. I put the book down and looked out of the train window. Through my tears I saw, rising above the trees in the distance, the towers and steeples of Kelham Hall, and a tremendous sense of loss washed over me.

Kelham Hall, a few miles outside Newark, had once been the home of a religious order, the Society of the Sacred Mission, which used it as a theological college to train boys for the Anglican priesthood. I went there in 1948, aged 14, and it was my home for eight important years. It had been built by George Gilbert Scott as the new country seat of the Manners–Sutton family in 1861. Scott had been hired to make minor alterations to the previous house, built in 1728–31, but on the night of 26 November 1857 it was gutted by fire. In *The Victorian Country House,* Mark Girouard says the fire was a piece of luck for Scott. Presented with an empty site and a compliant patron with a bulging purse, Scott created an astonishing building. Girouard says:

> The resulting phoenix of hard red brick that emerged from the ashes still surprises travellers who cross the River Trent at Kelham; and its amazing silhouette enriches the view for miles around.[5]

The Society bought Kelham in 1903, and added to Scott's Victorian Gothic building a great chapel, completed in 1928. It was a vast open space with four great arches that supported a magnificent dome. The dominating feature of the chapel was the massive bridge of the sanctuary arch, upon which stood an enormous crucifixion scene, created by Sargent Jagger, the sculptor of the Artillery Memorial at Hyde Park Corner. The huge Christ figure on the rood dominated the chapel. He was roped as well as nailed to the cross, and his brooding eyes followed one. I dreamed about Kelham chapel for years after I left, and the eyes of the Christ figure still haunt me.

The Society left Kelham in 1973, and the figures from the rood were installed in a garden in Milton Keynes. Kelham itself is now the headquarters of Newark District Council. The chapel, which its new owners market as 'The Dome', has its own events manager and is hired out for special functions. I went back a few years ago to make a television programme. The evening I was there the chapel was being used as a venue for the retirement party of the local fire chief. The fifty people present seemed lost in the great space, though they were doing their best to be cheerful among the scatter of tables. Above them stretched the bridge of the sanctuary arch, emptied now of the grieving figures that once stood there, and a tremendous sense of absence pervaded the place. As I tried to call back an echo of the plainsong that once filled the chapel with longing for the undiscovered beauty of God, I was suddenly filled with a fierce and sorrowful anger at the loss of what had once been a place of such dignity and purpose. Now, whenever I am on the train between Edinburgh and King's Cross, I look out of the window as we leave Newark to catch a glimpse of Kelham's towers and steeples, rising above the distant trees, and mourn.

Mourning lost time

What are we mourning when we mourn the destruction of things we have loved and the passing of time? Gerard Manley Hopkins says we are mourning ourselves, mourning our transience:

> Márgarét, are you gríeving
> Over Goldengrove unleaving?
> It is the blight man was born for,
> It is Margaret you mourn for.[6]

We know that nothing lasts, yet the sudden awareness of our own finitude can surprise us into grief. There are words and places and snatches of music that overwhelm us with regret at the gliding away of the years and the remembrance of what they have taken from us. There is a road I know, from a deep hollow by a river up to the top of a rising hill. I would always turn at the top to look at a range of mountains, misty in the distance, and the beauty of it always made me mourn. I think it was because my mother used to remember walking up another hill with us when we were children. When we grew up, the walking ceased, but she was never happier, she said, than in those days. Dylan Thomas in his most famous poem 'Do not go Gentle into that Good Night' described

> Wild men who caught and sang the sun in flight,
> And learn, too late, they grieved it on its way.[7]

I suspect that this is the melancholy truth that lies behind the conservative temperament and its determination to hold on to the things it knows and loves. The torrents of time wash so many things away from us that we long for some things to endure, especially the good things we ourselves have discovered or created. Even left-wingers are not immune to the charm of ancient traditions and the institutions that enshrine them, which is why many a horny-handed trade unionist has contentedly ended his days wrapped in ermine, lolling on the benches of the House of Lords, that first-class departure lounge for the great and the good of Britain. Fidelity is the great virtue of the conservative mind. It holds steadily to the people and institutions it loves and thereby provides more fickle souls with a sense of stability and security.

Holding on

In certain moods I not only feel the attractiveness of this conservative attitude to life, I profoundly sympathise with the moral imperative that lies behind it. Why not try to protect some of the things we have loved from what Shakespeare called 'cormorant devouring Time'? Time will get us all in the end, but why appease the monster, why not resist him, why not disdain the dizzy multitude who dance to his tune? In his exhilaratingly pessimistic book *Straw Dogs*, John Gray is very unflattering about the human animal, whose incessant discontent he sees as the greatest threat to the planet. He says that humans were probably at their most contented when they were hunter gatherers. With the invention of agriculture came surplus wealth and its oppressive distinctions; and with the invention of writing came the creation of mental abstractions, such as religious and political theories, that take their revenge upon their creators by tormenting them with unrealisable longings.[8] You don't have to agree with Gray's argument completely to acknowledge that humans are a problem to themselves. In us, reflective self-consciousness has a tendency to inflate and extend itself, which is why we end up having such a problem with the shifting flux of human history. The paradox is that we ourselves are the agents of the changes we find it so hard to adapt to and so difficult to keep up with. Just as we are getting used to the latest invention, the next one off the assembly line makes it obsolete. (You get used to working the VCR when along comes the DVD, after your son has gone to college and is no longer around to operate it for you.) We are constantly unsettled by our own cleverness and its ability to tear up the cultural environment and refashion it every generation, which is why we develop our own network of social and religious institutions that will be a bulwark against our addiction to change. And we fortify these citadels against devouring time with the double walls of revelation and tradition: 'It was God who gave us this system as a rampart against the chaos of our own restless hearts', we claim, 'and if we want to live peaceful and secure lives this is the way things must remain.' So a conservative attitude to the institutions we have built to protect us from the ravages of time seems to be wise as well as prudent. It is no accident that the conservative temperament is often associated with the religious attitude to life, the sense that important truths have been delivered to us for safe keeping from beyond ourselves so that they might protect us from ourselves. They give us a sense that here, at least, we are in possession of something that will endure, what R.S. Thomas called 'the glimpsed good place permanent'.[9] Even Jesus was not immune to this sense that the old ways were precious and should not be lightly abandoned: 'No man having drunk old wine straightway desireth new: for he saith, The old is better.'[10]

But there are always difficulties with the institutions and traditions that the past has bequeathed to us. The first is that someone, somewhere has to pay for the upkeep of these bulwarks against change, and it is rarely the persons who derive the most benefit from them. There are always injustices, sometimes implicit, sometimes explicit, in these fortifying systems that gradually corrupt them and which, if ignored, finally threaten their survival. Behind the reverent appeal to changeless tradition there can lie something much uglier, which is the ruthless determination to hold onto power for its own sake. This is the moral paradox that lies at the heart of conservatism. We create and increasingly revere the institutions that guard us against the floodwaters of time, yet change is the law of our nature and the hope of change is often the only thing that keeps people going in difficult days. Reflective consciousness, which curses us with its restless quest for the new, also blesses us through discoveries that improve our lives. Any who doubt this only have to imagine themselves back to the time before the discovery of anaesthesia.

The melancholy truth is that we are life's passing guests who will soon have to make way for the next house party, and if we try to resist our own leaving we only succeed in making ourselves more miserable. The art of living well has a lot to do with knowing when it's time to go, so that we can gather up our things and get on the bus before the new guests arrive. And this is true for institutions as well as individuals. They, too, are transient and have to adapt to the way the next generation wants to operate.

Refusing to adapt to this dynamic principle of constant becoming is usually fatal to the resistant institution. Sociologists describe this kind of institutional immobilism as *morphological fundamentalism*. Another paradox is that it is usually the unfaithful, the radicals and romantics, whom Rumi the Sufi poet called 'lovers of leaving', who secure the survival of human institutions by inoculating them with a foretaste of the future that is about to overwhelm them. It is their inability to commit themselves for life to anything except the restless quest for something better that enables heretics to introduce the faithful conservative majority to new and different ways of doing things. By denouncing the injustices of the past and proclaiming the superiority of the future, they prepare society for what is coming. The dissident's refusal to conform to received standards helps to save humanity from the ultimate stupidity of holding out forever against the emergence of new social realities. There are many examples of this law at work, but the most potent of them is the emancipation of women.

Until fairly recently, the dominant institutions in our society, the great carriers of tradition, were completely male dominated. As is the way with all traditional constructs, this male dominance was not considered to be culturally incidental, a passing phase; it was held to be a permanent reality that was part of the intrinsic nature of the institutions in question. Male dominance was sanctioned by divine revelation and ancient tradition. But there came a point in the evolution of the status of women when this male intransigence began to look not strong and competent, but stupid. The question 'Why?' that was ceaselessly put to the conventional power structure by the women's movement began to make the constant reply *because this is the way it has always been* look increasingly silly. In time, men realised what idiots they were, and changes began to be made, changes that have cumulatively created a radical social revolution in my lifetime. This has happened in every area of life, except in traditional religious institutions. Incidentally, one of the advantages of still having these conservative forms of religion around is so that we can point to them as living exhibits in history's museum of ancient cultures. If your glorious eighteen-year-old daughter, who refuses to be patronised by any mere male of the species, really wants to know 'what it was like in the olden days, Mummy', you don't have to invest in time travel to show her the dismal truth; there are plenty of old religions around that will do the job just as well.

But I need to offer a balancing observation here. When I talk about the radical questioning of human institutions that prompts them to evolve and adapt to the future, I am not claiming that this process always secures moral progress or human happiness. I do believe that the emancipation of women was not only an irresistible social development; it was also a considerable moral improvement on what went before. It has helped us to humanise and banish much of the cruelty that was endemic in many of our social structures. In 1995 Margaret Forster wrote a book called *Hidden Lives*. It was a piece of research into the women in her own working-class family at the beginning of the twentieth century. She ended the book with these words:

> All the women whose lives and times I have touched upon would have been able to fulfil themselves in an entirely different and much more gratifying way if they could have benefited from the radical changes

in the last half century from which I have benefited.
Let no one say nothing has changed, that women
have it as bad as ever. They do not. My personal
curiosity may not have been satisfied but my larger
curiosity, as to whether life has indeed improved for
women like my immediate ancestors, is. And I am
glad, glad not to have been born a working-class girl
in 1869 or 1901. Everything, for a woman, is better
now, even if it is still not as good as it could be. To
forget or deny that is an insult to the women who
have gone before.[11]

But social change always has its losses as well as its
gains. It constantly robs people of things they have
grown to love and value. This is why conservatives
mourn the loss of the traditional family unit, which
has been the most conspicuous casualty of female
emancipation, though the reasons for its collapse are
complex. The balancing observation must be that the
traditional family had a bleak and frequently brutal
downside. The point to be grasped here is that, given
our restless nature as a species, social change is a constant; so the issue is not whether to accept or reject
it, but how best to use it. By refusing to engage with
change, by refusing to question the effectiveness or

justice of received traditions, we not only endanger their survival, we may seriously corrupt them. There comes a point in the defence of the received system when it may become not just stupid to go on doing things the old way, but seriously damaging to the health of the human community. Skilful living is more an art than a science. We should be more intent on imparting to our children the kind of emotional confidence that will enable them to adapt to the changes their lives will encounter than in arming them with fixed and solid certainties that are likely to collapse under the pressure of events. I have already suggested that the best way to do this is to nurture in them the ability to improvise that is the genius of the jazz musician. It follows, of course, that they must first master the tradition, learn the rules of play, in order to have the confidence to abandon them when the situation requires it. They can then give themselves over to the music and let it play itself through them. I think that is a suggestive model for human living. It calls us to a certain lightness of being, an ability to adapt, to move, so that we can change elegantly rather than awkwardly when the time is ripe.

The wistful side of this is that each generation has to learn all over again how and when to hand over responsibility to new players and retire to the sidelines. And we have to find the grace to do this at the very time in our lives when we are at our least resilient and may be mourning the fading of our powers. There is no sadder spectacle than the person who tries to cling to the baton long after their course has been completed. But even this is understandable. There is an inevitable poignancy as the end of life approaches. When you are young and the future is filled with unknown promise, it is much easier to celebrate the fact that life is in a constant state of becoming rather than in a permanent state of being. It is a different matter when you realise that, almost without noticing it, you have become old and that soon the incessant movement of life will carry you away, as it has carried away every generation since the human species crawled out of the primeval slime. As we look back, we agree with Job that our lives were swifter than a weaver's shuttle. So, adapting to increasing age and learning to accept the inevitability of death are the final spiritual challenges that confront us.

Packing for the trip

But it is difficult not to be depressed by the prospect of leaving this earth. We feel that just as we are getting the hang of the game and have wised up sufficiently to understand how to play it well, the whistle goes and the game ends. It is not surprising that Dylan Thomas advised us to 'rage against the dying of the light'.[12] But the universe is not interested in our complaint. The mournful fact is that life is indifferent to our fate; it is programmed to care for the species, never for the individual; and, without death, life as we know it would be insupportable.

> To obviate the absolute necessity of death, the reproduction of living things would have had to cease soon after it began. The consequence of this would be the absence of all growth, all evolution of the species. Man, the result of a long evolutionary process, would never have appeared on earth, or would never have evolved to his present state. In a word, we can conceive of the absence of death only in an entirely static universe where a determined number of members of different species would have been created in the beginning and remained constant for the duration. I do not know whether such

a universe would have been preferable to our own. But there is no doubt that in an evolutionary universe death is a necessity.[13]

Death is a necessity, and its necessity is spiritual as well as physical. Without the final boundary of death there would be little to spur human achievement, because there would always be time to get round to it later. Maybe that is why Jesus told us to work while it was yet day, for the night was coming when no one could work. Dying is our final work and, like everything else, we can do it well or badly. Fortunately, life provides us with many opportunities to rehearse our own dying. As well as the death of relationships and the ending of careers, we are constant witnesses to the slow dying of movements and traditions. In contemplating our own decline or the decline of institutions we love, T.S. Eliot is as good a guide as any:

> Let me disclose the gifts reserved for age,
> To set a crown upon your lifetime's effort.
> First, the cold friction of expiring sense
> Without enchantment, offering no promise
> But bitter tastelessness of shadow fruit
> As body and soul begin to fall asunder.[14]

Physical decline, 'the cold friction of expiring sense', is the inescapable prelude to dying. It would be much easier if we were just switched off like a light: one minute here, the next minute gone. Unfortunately, it rarely happens like that. Unless we die violently, from an internal or external assault to the system, most of us run down gradually, and we are all too aware when it starts to happen. Black humour is the most engaging response to physical decline, as body and soul begin to fall asunder. When he was in his nineties, my father-in-law used to joke that he'd stopped buying green bananas. And he enjoyed the crack about the old man who after seeing an attractive woman walking down the street found his pace-maker opened the garage door. My favourite death joke is a monologue by an American comedian George Carlin:

> The most unfair thing about life is the way it ends. I mean, life is tough. It takes up a lot of your time. What do you get at the end of it? A death. What's that, a bonus? I think the life cycle is all backwards. You should die first, get it out of the way. Then you live in an old age home. You get kicked out when you're too young, you get a gold watch, you go to

work. You work forty years till you're young enough to enjoy your retirement. You do drugs, alcohol, you party, you get ready for high school. You go to grade school, you become a kid, you play, you have no responsibilities, you become a little baby, you go back into the womb, you spend your last nine months floating . . . you finish off as an orgasm.

Apart from humour, another source of consolation in old age is that vanity can sometimes fall away to be replaced by an amused affection for the engaging varieties of human folly, not excluding your own. In his autobiography *Self Consciousness*, John Updike muses on how embarrassed he used to be at the awful hats his father wore when he was in his sixties; yet he now finds himself, having arrived at that time of life himself, wearing exactly the same kind of battered monstrosities. It is possible to say a rueful 'Yes' to our fading energies, and begin to appreciate the humour and understanding that old age can bring.

The saddest part of aging is the complete disintegration that many undergo, sometimes spending long joyless years in bed, impatiently waiting for

death to take them. It is captured in a poem by Gail
Holst-Warhaft:

> In the end is the body – what we know
> as inspiration departs before
> the final assault of pain and decay.
> Even the carpenter's son from Nazareth
> could not, in the end, overcome
> the body's claims though he knew
> inspiration more than most.
>
> And don't imagine his mother
> was indifferent to the hammer smashing
> the arrangement of bone and sinew she
> had held in hers at the beginning.
> She wished him back unpierced, smelling
> of sawdust and sweat. He was the one
> she'd hoped would close her eyes in the end.
>
> In the end my mother lay
> body-bound, curled like a foetus,
> fretting for a peppermint, a sip of whisky,
> the pillow turned this way and that,
> and she a woman who, buoyant in silk
> and shingled hair, stood on the hill
> at Fiesole reciting her Browning to the wind.[15]

One of the cruellest side-effects of the sophistication of present-day society is that we have perfected ways of keeping people alive long after any pleasure or meaning has gone from their lives. We sentence them to years of mournful inanition, though many of them would happily take their leave while they had a mind to do so. There is a sweetness and a mercy in allowing people to choose the moment of their own passing from the earth. The prohibition on mercy killing in our society is one of the most powerful residues of Christianity, which holds that our lives are not ours to dispose of, but are given to us by God, who alone can establish the time of their ending. In his discussion of euthanasia in his book *What is Good*, A.C. Grayling points out that in Imperial Rome assisting at someone's suicide was considered a merciful act. He goes on:

> Christian ethics brought about a complete change in the acceptability of such practices. The idea that life is sacred because 'god-given' introduces a proscription on the taking of life that has been construed in blanket terms when viewed from the perspective of practices such as abortion, infanticide and euthanasia (and inconsistently) it has otherwise

admitted of many exceptions, such as war, killing in self-defence, and the execution of criminals and heretics. Nor has there ever been a principled extension of the 'sanctity of life' thesis to non-human creatures (using 'creature' in the theological sense to denote something brought into existence, and in the case of animals given conscious life, by a deity), despite the fact that the grounds for proscribing killing in the human and non-human cases are identical – unless one adds theses about souls as inhabiting only human animals.[16]

We would expect that in a truly multi-traditional society both the Christian proscription on suicide and secular sympathy towards those who want to avail themselves of it would be tolerated. As the Christian view of life becomes an increasingly minority perspective, we shall gradually become open to the compassion of allowing people to take their leave of life with dignity when they choose to do so, and not just when indifferent nature decides.

Rage at human folly

Eliot's next words in 'Little Gidding' are all too predictive of what happens to many people in later life.

If they are not careful they become unattractive and angry old reactionaries. Let me repeat the verse so far, adding the next three lines:

> Let me disclose the gifts reserved for age,
> To set a crown upon your lifetime's effort.
> First, the cold friction of expiring sense
> Without enchantment, offering no promise
> But bitter tastelessness of shadow fruit
> As body and soul begin to fall asunder.
> Second, the conscious impotence of rage
> At human folly, and the laceration
> Of laughter at what ceases to amuse.

I am not quite over the hill myself, but I have noticed in some of my elderly friends that their understandable love of the old ways has mutated into an ugly and contemptuous hatred of the new. Given the accelerating rate of change in today's world, it is hardly surprising that the old, whether in age or in attitude, can become increasingly hostile towards a society they no longer feel at home in. Behind their harrumphing at the strangeness and excess of contemporary manners there probably lies an unacknowledged sadness at their own declining powers, as well as the fading of institutions they cherish and the recognition that a new and unsympathetic generation is taking over from them. This anguish is particularly keen in Britain at the moment for those who witness with sadness the decline of the Christian churches. 'The allure of lost consequence and faded power . . . the passing of time, the passing of friends' seduced Jan Morris into an attractive melancholy; but they can prompt some people into that 'impotence of rage at human folly' that Eliot describes ironically as one of the gifts reserved for age. Bitter old people are an ugly and depressing spectacle, as they fulminate against the degradation of society and the inferiority of young people today. The irony is that literature shows just how enduring a human characteristic bitterness is. There have been people throughout history who have complained about how everything is going to hell in a handcart, and how ungrateful or undisciplined the new generation is. Their rhetoric of irritated abuse is surprisingly consistent down the ages. In the century before the birth of Christ, the Roman poet Horace captured the characteristics of the grumpy reactionary for all time:

> Tiresome, complaining, a praiser of the times that
> were when he was a boy, a castigator and censor of
> the young generation. The years as they come bring
> a lot of advantage with them, but as they go by they
> take a lot away too . . . What do the ravages of time
> not injure? Our parents' age (worse than our grand-
> parents') has produced us, more worthless still, who
> will soon give rise to a yet more vicious generation.[17]

Knowing how easy it is to descend into this lacerating frame of mind, we should struggle to achieve a
more imaginative response to the new and different.
Having had our place in the sun, we should rejoice
that others are now replacing us. History suggests that
our successors will do some things well and some
things badly, exactly like every other generation.

The characteristic of Western society that is
probably most difficult for conservative people to
adjust to is its pluralism, both ethically and ethni-
cally. I have already explored the relatively new fact
that Western society has many cultures and value
systems. Humans are wanderers, in ideas as well as
in space. When we wander we mix with and enrich
one another, but the freshly minted combinations
are difficult for people with entrenched attitudes to

deal with. The crisis in the British Conservative
Party is an instructive example of this phenomenon.
After its comprehensive defeat in two general elec-
tions, it went in for some radical soul-searching. The
burden of its analysis was that it was like an elderly
person who was unable to adapt to the way the
world had changed. Some of the party's thinkers
pointed out that unless it began to accept the nature
of the new Britain, not grudgingly, but with enthu-
siasm, then its present decline would end in one of
those deaths that the history of institutions is littered
with. The irony is that the Conservative Party, for
most of its history, has been the pragmatic party par
excellence, able to adapt to changes in culture and
society with enormous versatility, cheerfully stealing
the clothes and ideas of its rivals. Enduring institutions, like people who have lived a long time, have
already shown considerable versatility in adapting to
the challenges and changes that have confronted
them in life, so it is sad when they completely lose
that resilience at the end. There can be a subtle pleasure in the melancholy awareness that life is leaving
us behind, but we don't have to fall into that cor-
rosive hatred of the new and the different that

too-often disfigures the human scene. The best antidote to this kind of bitterness is to remember our
own youthful follies and mistakes. Magnanimity
and tolerance should be the hallmark of old age, not
bigotry and bitterness.

Remorse

The final section quoted from Eliot's 'Little Gidding'
may offer us a clue about how to achieve this tolerance. It goes on:

> And last, the rending pain of re-enactment
> of all that you have done and been; the shame
> of motives late revealed, and the awareness
> of things ill done and done to others' harm
> which once you took for exercise of virtue.
> Then fools' approval stings, and honour stains.
> From wrong to wrong the exasperated spirit
> Proceeds, unless restored by that refining fire
> Where you must move in measure, like a dancer.

'The rending path of re-enactment of all that you
have done and been' is the saddest aspect of the
interior life of the old. There is an inevitable

tendency, when we look back on our lives, to con-
centrate on our failures and mistakes, wrong roads
taken, right roads not taken. That's when shame
burns, and we are tempted to feel that we have done
little or nothing with our life. It may be that the
great monsters of human history should feel this
kind of lacerating shame, but, generally speaking,
wallowing in our mistakes is wrong and shows an
ungrateful lack of balance. This may be another
toxic residue from Christianity. There has been a
tendency in the Christian tradition to emphasise
human sinfulness; and penitence has certainly had a
disproportionate role in liturgy and private devo-
tion. The best theologians have always been aware
of this tendency. My confessor once ordered me,
after a particularly mournful recitation of my sins,
to come back next time and make an act of thanks-
giving for the things I had done well. Certainly, self-
knowledge is important if we are to live honestly,
but we should find the kind of balance that allows
us to acknowledge our good points as well as our
bad. The real motive for self-examination is not so
that we can convict ourselves of being miserable
sinners, but so that we can grow in self-knowledge

in order to be able to modify the damaging effect we may have had on other people. Socrates said that the unexamined life is not worth living; we could also say that the unexamined life is not worth dying, either. When taking stock, we should be honest about what we have done badly, making every effort, before it is too late, to mend relationships we have damaged; but we should also affirm what we have done well in our journey through life. Most lives have had their share of sorrow and endurance, but they are an achievement nevertheless. And we ought to acknowledge that there was a certain givenness about our lives that was not of our choosing. We played the hand we were dealt at birth. It is a mysterious fact that not only were some people given better cards than others, but some of them were better at playing the game. Nietzsche said that the strong are good at self-forgetting and self-forgiving because they do not allow their own failings and frailties to assume a dominant role in their consciousness. In the energetic living of any life, mistakes will be made, but we should not allow them to derail us from our good purposes; nor should we allow the memory of them to obscure the record of the satisfactions life has brought us. That's why I like the tone of Raymond Carver's short poem 'Late Fragment':

> And did you get what
> you wanted from this life, even so?
> I did.
> And what did you want?
> To call myself beloved, to feel myself
> beloved on the earth.[18]

Checking out

In the poem 'Aubade' that I quoted at the beginning of this book, Philip Larkin described death as 'the sure extinction that we travel to and shall be lost in always'. Its prospect frightened him:

> – no sight, no sound,
> No touch or taste or smell, nothing to think with,
> Nothing to love or link with,
> The anaesthetic from which none come round.

But what is the nature of this fear and is death its true object? I can still remember vividly the moment that

death became a personal fact for me, and an object of
fear. It was during one of the long summers of the
Second World War, days of double summertime, when
it was light till midnight in the town where I lived in
the west of Scotland. There was a war on and a lot of
the men were away, but the real horror of that summer for those of us on the home front was an out-
break of viral meningitis among children. There was
a panic in the towns in the area. The public swimming pool was closed down because it was thought
the virus was carried in the water. I remember the
anxiety of the mothers in our street and my own
increasing awareness that we were all at risk. Then
death came to the house opposite, to a boy we knew
called Peter, whose father worked on the railway.
Peter was twelve when he died, and his was the first
death I had registered. I can still remember the grief
and fear in our street. That was the moment I realised
we were always old enough to die.

> From a proud tower in the town,
> Death looked gigantically down.[19]

In thinking about what St Paul called 'humanity's

last enemy', we ought to begin by making a distinction between dying and death. The process of
dying can indeed be frightening. Apart from the
physical pain that may accompany it, something that
can usually be alleviated chemically, there are two
elements in the experience that can make it spiritually alarming. The most obvious and immediate is
the pain of having to leave forever those we love. We
only have to recall the memory of other separations
to realise how wrenching this can be. History is
drenched in the memory of these departures, all
experienced as a kind of dying: the frail figure
watching the car disappear round the bend before
turning in at the door; the moment at the airport
when we can't say goodbye because our heart seems
to be filling our throat and we clutch hands and turn
away. Painful as most of these partings are, there is
usually the promise of future meetings to console us;
and there are ways of keeping in touch with people
we love that can, to some extent, compensate us for
their absence. But in dying we face the final and
absolute separation, the immediate prospect of which
can be devastating, especially if it is untimely and we
are being cut down in the prime of life. In dying we

lose the future, our own future, as well as the future of those we love.

So it is easy to see why death is thought of as the last enemy, the agent of ultimate, irrecoverable loss. This is one reason why the medical profession used to practise the kindly deceit of keeping the knowledge of impending death from their patients. That is less the case today, because strong people insist on being present at their own dying, so that they can do it right. To die consciously and well takes courage, but it is the correct thing to do, if we can pull it off. Apart from anything else, dying well is an act of love towards those we leave behind, because it helps them to deal with the reality of our going from them. Fortitude has been described as the most important of the virtues, because it is the one on which the others are based. One reason why it is good to practise fortitude in life is so that it will be available to us when we are dying, though gratitude should be present as well. Naturally, we are sad to leave the party while it is still in full swing, but we had a good enough time while we were there, so we should bow out graciously and depart without fuss when the carriage comes for us at midnight.

Apart from sorrow at leaving, the other pain that

may be experienced by the dying is fear of what might come after. Religion has been highly productive of this kind of anxiety, particularly Christianity, with its diseased and ugly doctrine of Hell. The healthy antidote to this kind of anguish, for those who can take it, is not false assurance about the bliss that awaits us in the next life, but the recognition that, though dying may be painful, death won't be, because it is our old friend Nothing. Paul Celan taught us, at our beginning, to praise Nothing for the brief joy of life. Now, at our ending, we can praise Nothing for the blessed oblivion into which we shall return. Death is the term we use to describe the dissolution of the physical elements we were made of and their return to the earth from which they came, but we aren't going to be there to witness it. According to the philosopher Epicurus, to fear the non-existence that follows our dying is as irrational as regretting that we did not exist before we were conceived and born. A.C. Grayling puts it like this:

> Those who fear death perform an impossible feat: they imagine themselves witnessing their own non-existence, and lamenting it.[20]

That is what Larkin was doing in his famous poem 'Aubade'. It is an understandable but unnecessary anxiety. There was a long time when we were not; then there was a brief time when we were; and again there will be a long time when we no longer are. We are passing guests on earth, like the 60 billion human beings who preceded us.[21]

> Earth said to Death
> Give these a little breath
> Give them eight days.
> Eight days to feel the sun,
> To see the limes in leaf,
> Eight days . . .
> Myself I ask no stay,
> Mine is a longer day,
> But theirs is brief.
>
> Who rives me, does but plough my field for grain
> But these, I cannot make them live again.
>
> Give me eight days
> And I will pour the silence of June
> Into this April noon.
> Wine of October in the vine still curled,
> Then let you come.

Darkness shall find their sleeping undismayed.
Who shall make them afraid
Who saw eternity
In the brief compass of an April day?[22]

A sentence is not finished till it has a full stop, and every life needs a dying to complete it. It is dying that finishes us, that ends our story. At the end of *The English Patient*, when Almásy carries Katherine Clifton into the desert, Michael Ondaatje captures something of the way death finally defines us.

We die containing a richness of lovers and tribes, tastes we have swallowed, bodies we have plunged into and swum up as if rivers of wisdom, characters we have climbed into as if trees, fears we have hidden in as if caves. I wish for all this to be marked on my body when I am dead. I believe in such cartography . . .[23]

When the map of our life is complete, and we die in the richness of our own history, some among the living will miss us for a while, but the earth will go on without us. Its day is longer than ours, though we now know that it too will die. Our brief finitude is but a beautiful spark in the vast darkness of space. So we should live the fleeting day with passion and, when the night comes, depart from it with grace.

Afterword

One of the obvious truisms about the craft of authoring books is that writers have to be attentive readers of the works of other writers. While this is also true in the case of writers of fiction, it is probably more obvious to the writers and readers of non-fiction – and how I wish we had a positive way of describing that category instead of having to use that hyphenated negative. In my own case it is obvious that my books have all been conversations with other writers, which is why a young friend once complained to me that my earlier attempts were only strings of quotations loosely connected by me. I pleaded guilty to that charge and informed her that I was trying to write the kind of books I liked to read. Not having a very systematic mind, I enjoyed the serendipitous side of reading because of the way it introduced me to other writers whom I would not otherwise have discovered for myself. The books I have enjoyed most have had this conversational quality, not unlike a long evening by the fireside with a group of friends, including some I have only just met, who are all interested in chasing ideas round the room. A good book gathers you into interesting company and gets you following thoughts you may never have encountered before.

Skimming back through some of the books I have written over the years, even the ones that now embarrass me, I am moved by the way they remind me of what I was reading at the time. They are like reading old journals that take me suddenly back to the now of then. Reading obituaries of writers who influenced me a lifetime ago has the same effect, which is probably why I have always been moved by William Cory's translation of an epigram by Callimachus:

> They told me, Heraclitus, they told me you were dead,
> They brought me bitter news to hear and bitter tears to shed.
> I wept as I remembered how often you and I
> Had tired the sun with talking and sent him down the sky.

Of all the books I have written, *Looking in the Distance*, though it is one of the shortest, is the one that owes most to other writers, the majority of them poets. It may not be widely understood outside the business that writers have to pay to quote other writers in their books, and poetry, unless it's out of copyright, can be pricey. When it came out, paying for permissions for *Looking in the Distance* cost me more than for any other book I have published, but I did not grudge a penny of it. At the time it was the most personal of my books and

I wrote it to show that even if the practice of religion was fading in our culture this did not have to mean the eclipse of our spiritual life. My own experience of this shift in spiritual perspective happened to gather round the kind of reading I was doing. As a priest for over forty years I had had to practise a kind of reading called *lectio divina*, which meant spending time every morning and evening reading from the Bible, with a particular emphasis on the psalms that enabled me to read all one hundred and fifty of them every month.

Frankly, I had always found this a bit of a chore, but it became an even heavier duty as my own difficulties with religion increased. Something told me I had to abandon the discipline without losing the benefit it had brought to my soul over the years; but what could I replace it with? The obvious answer was poetry, read as systematically as I had read the Bible, so that is what I started to do. I liked the fact that there was still a tinge of obligation about it. Even more I liked what I came to think of as the sacramental nature of poetry. In the Christian sacramental tradition, it is believed that certain acts, such as the sharing of bread and wine together, show rather than tell us something important about the human condition. I had always found Christianity too talkative, with its constant offering of explanations that did not explain; but I had always been moved by the way, when it stopped talking and started acting, it sometimes enabled me to enter an experience larger than myself. At its best, poetry also has this sacramental character: it does not so much talk about human experience as make it present in a way that allows us to enter it. Like all good art, poetry does not tell, it shows. That is why there is so much poetry in this book.

One of the dangers we face in our largely post-religious culture is that we might lose what's good in religion as well as what's bad. Disciplined reflection is good for us. Opening ourselves to the sorrows of others is good for us. Understanding the diversity of human experience is good for us. These may be grand ambitions, but they were my motives for writing this book. My consolation for its inevitable failure is that in reading it you may have discovered other writers, some of them poets, with whom to take the conversation further.

RICHARD HOLLOWAY
EDINBURGH, 2019

NOTES

I: Looking

1. A.S.J.Tessimond, *The Collected Poems*, ed. Hubert Nicholson, University of Reading Press, Reading 1985.
2. Friedrich Nietzsche, *On the Genealogy of Morals*, 3rd Essay, Section 17, in *Basic Writings of Nietzsche*, tr. and ed. Walter Kaufman, The Modern Library, New York 1992.
3. From *The Gift, Poems by Hafiz*, trans. Daniel Ladinsky, Penguin Compass Press, USA 1999
4. Yehuda Amichai, *Selected Poetry*, Faber and Faber, London 2000, p. 94.
5. Philip Larkin, 'Aubade', *Collected Poems*, Faber and Faber, London 1990, p. 208.
6. Paul Celan, *Poems of Paul Celan*, trans. Michael Hamburger, Anvil Press, 1995.
7. R.S.Thomas, *Collected Poems*, Dent, London 1993, p. 220.
8. Martin Rees, *Our Final Century*, Heinemann, London 2003, p. 99.
9. Antonio Damasio, *Looking for Spinoza,* Heinemann, London 2003.
10. Ibid., pp. 284–285.
11. Bill Bryson, *A Short History of Nearly Everything*, Doubleday, London and New York 2003, p. 115.
12. As quoted in Bryson, *A Short History*, p. 15.

13. Robinson Jeffers, *The Beginning and the End and Other Poems*, Random House, New York. Copyright © 1954, 1963 Garth Jeffers and Donnan Jeffers.

14. Friedrich Nietzsche, *Beyond Good and Evil*, Section 258, in *Basic Writings of Nietzsche*, The Modern Library, New York 1992, p. 392.

15. The Gospel of Luke, chapter 6, verses 24–25.

16. The Gospel of Mark, chapter 11, verses 15–17.

17. Gil Courtemanche, *A Sunday at the Pool in Kigali*, Canongate, Edinburgh 2003, p. 211.

18. Quoted in Richard Dawkins, *A Devil's Chaplain*, Weidenfeld and Nicolson, London 2003, p. 8.

19. Fyodor Dostoevsky, *The Karamazov Brothers*, Oxford World's Classics 1998, p. 308.

20. Sylvia Townsend Warner, *Selected Poems*, Carcanet Press, Manchester 1985.

21. Albert Camus, *The Plague*, Penguin, London 1960, p. 296.

22. Edward Hirsch, 'Simone Weil in Assissi', in *Burning Bright: An Anthology of Sacred Poetry*, ed. Patricia Hampl, Ballantine Books, New York 1995.

23. Miguel De Unamuno, *The Tragic Sense of Life*, Fontana, London 1962, p. 256.

II: Speaking

1. Donna Tartt, *The Little Friend*, Bloomsbury, London 1992, p. 3.

2. Stephen Jay Gould, *I Have Landed*, Jonathan Cape, London 2002, p. 55

3. Charles Freeman, *The Closing of the Western Mind*, Pimlico, London 2003, p. 20.

4. Ibid., p. 65.

5. John Updike, *Memories of the Ford Administration*, Penguin, London 1993, p. 296.
6. John Milton, *Paradise Lost*.
7. John Calvin, *Institutes of the Christian Religion*, The Calvin Translation Society, Edinburgh 1845, book 2, chapter 1.
8. Quoted by M. Warner, *Alone of All Her Sex*, Weidenfeld and Nicolson, London 1985, p. 57.
9. Calvin, *Institutes*, book 3, chapter 21.
10. Robert Burns, *Selected Poems*, Penguin, London 1993, p. 20.
11. James Hogg, *The Private Memoirs and Confessions of a Justified Sinner*, Canongate Classics, Edinburgh 1990, p. 100.
12. Ibid., p. 162.
13. Ibid., p. 164.
14. Ibid., p. 166.
15. Ibid., pp. 162ff.
16. Friedrich Nietzsche, *The Will to Power*, Vintage, New York 1968, p. 12.
17. T.S. Eliot, 'East Coker', in *The Complete Poems and Plays*, Harcourt Brace, New York 1952, p. 128.
18. Michel Houellebecq, *Atomised*, Vintage, London 2001, ibid., pp. 308ff.
19. John Updike, *Memories of the Ford Administration*, Penguin, London 1993, p. 296.
20. Book of Judges, chapter 17, verse 6.
21. Frederick Crews, 'Saving us from Darwin, Part 1', *The New York Review of Books*, 4 October 2001.
22. Stephen Dunn, *Sweetness: Staying Alive*, Bloodaxe, Tarset, Northumberland 2002, p. 121.
23. Cited in Isaiah Berlin, *The Proper Study of Mankind*, Chatto and Windus, London 1997, p. 524.

24. Annie Dillard, *Holy the Firm*, Harper and Row, New York 1984, p. 56.
25. A.S.J.Tessimond, *The Collected Poems,* University of Reading Press, Reading 1985.

III: Listening

1. *The Portable Enlightenment Reader*, ed. Isaac Kramnick, Penguin, New York 1995, p. 267.
2. Book of Genesis, chapter 19, verses 5 and 8.
3. Andrew Wheatcroft, *Infidels*, Penguin Viking. London 2003, p. 189.
4. Aristotle, *Nichomachean Ethics*, 1155a3, in *Introduction to Aristotle*, The Modern Library, New York 1947, p. 471.
5. Antonio Damasio, *Looking for Spinoza*, Heinemann, London 2003, p. 40.
6. Richard Holloway, *Godless Morality*, Canongate, Edinburgh 1999.
7. *Kind of Blue*, Miles Davis, Columbia CD.
8. For a full discussion of this, see Ashley Kahn, *Kind of Blue: The Making of the Miles Davis Masterpiece*, Granta, London 2002.
9. Friedrich Nietzsche, *Daybreak,* Cambridge University Press 1982, paragraph 76, pp. 45–46.
10. Simone Weil, *Gravity and Grace*, Routledge & Kegan Paul, London 1987, p. 58.
11. Edmund Burke, *Reflections on the Revolution in France*, Harvard Classics, New York 2001.
12. Sigmund Freud, *Civilization and its Discontents,* in *Civilization, Society and Religion*, Penguin, London 1991, pp. 262, 265.
13. Quoted in the *Guardian*, 14th September 2000.
14. Quoted in the *Guardian*, as above.

15. John Stuart Mill, *On Liberty*, Penguin Classics, London 1985, chapter 2.
16. Susan Greenfield, *Tomorrow's People*, Penguin, London 2003, p. 115.
17. Martin Rees, *Our Final Century*, Heinemann, London 2003, p. 12.
18. John Rawls, *A Theory of Justice*, revised edition, Oxford University Press, Oxford 1999, p. 15.

IV: Leaving

1. Psalm 91, Verse 10.
2. Jan Morris, *Trieste and the Meaning of Nowhere*, Faber and Faber, London 2002, pp. 3–4.
3. Victor Maskell is partly modelled on the Irish poet, Louis MacNeice, the son of a Church of Ireland bishop. MacNeice's mother died when he was a child, an emotional shock that marked him for life. He remembers it in his poem 'Autobiography' (in *Collected Poems*, Faber and Faber, London 1991, p. 183):

   > When I was five the black dreams came;
   > Nothing after was quite the same.
   > *Come back early or never come.*

4. John Banville, *The Untouchable*, Picador, London 1997, pp. 243ff.
5. Mark Girouard, *The Victorian Country House*, Yale University Press, New Haven and London 1979.
6. Gerard Manley Hopkins, 'Spring and Fall, to a Young Child', in *Poems*, Oxford University Press, London 1948, p. 94.
7. Dylan Thomas, 'Do not go Gentle into that Good Night', in *The Poems*, J.M. Dent, London 1974, p. 208.

8. John Gray, *Straw Dogs*, Granta, London 2002, p. 157.
9. Quoted by Margaret Drabble in *A Writer's Britain*, Thames and Hudson, London 1979, p. 264.
10. Gospel of Luke, chapter 5, verse 39.
11. Margaret Forster, *Hidden Lives*, Penguin, London 1995.
12. Dylan Thomas, 'Do not go Gentle into that Good Night'.
13. Ignace Lepp, *Death and its Mysteries*, Burns and Oates, London 1969, p. 7.
14. T.S. Eliot, 'Little Gidding', in *The Complete Poems and Plays*, Harcourt Brace, New York 1952, p. 141.
15. Gail Holst-Warhaft, 'In the End is the Body', in *The Gospels in our Image*, ed. David Curzon, Harcourt Brace, New York 1995, p. 253.
16. A.C. Grayling, *What is Good?* Weidenfeld and Nicolson, London 2003, p. 178.
17. Horace, *Ars Poetica* 173, 45.
18. Raymond Carver, *All of Us: Collected Poems*, Harvill Press, New York 1996.
19. Edgar Allan Poe 'The City in the Sea' in *The Works of the Late Edgar Allan Poe*, vol. II, ed. Rufus Wilmot Ainswold, J.S. Redfield, New York, 1850–56.
20. A.C. Grayling, *What is Good?*, p. 40. (I am also grateful to Professor Grayling for the quote from Epicurus.)
21. Martin Rees, *Our Final Century*, Heinemann, London 2003, p. 136.
22. Helen Waddell, 'Earth said to Death', in Monica Blackett, *The Mark of the Maker: a Portrait of Helen Waddell*, Constable, London 1973, p. 141.
23. Michael Ondaatje, *The English Patient*, Picador, London 1993, p. 261.

SELECT BIBLIOGRAPHY

Amichai, Yehuda, *Selected Poetry,* Faber and Faber, London 2000

Banville, John, *The Untouchable,* Picador, London 1997

Berlin, Isaiah, *The Proper Study of Mankind,* Chatto and Windus, London 1997

Blackett, Monica, *The Mark of the Maker: a Portrait of Helen Waddell,* Constable, London 1973

Bryson, Bill, *A Short History of Nearly Everything,* Doubleday, London and New York 2003

Burns, Robert, *Selected Poems,* Penguin, London 1993

Camus, Albert, *The Plague,* Penguin, London 1960

Carver, Raymond, *All of Us: Collected Poems,* Harvill Press, New York, 1996

Celan, Paul, *Selected Poems,* Penguin, London 1995

Courtemanche, Gil, *A Sunday at the Pool in Kigali,* Canongate, Edinburgh 2003

Crews, Frederick, 'Saving us from Darwin, Part 1', *The New York Review of Books,* 4 October 2001

Damasio, Antonio, *Looking for Spinoza,* Heinemann, London 2003

Dawkins, Richard, *A Devil's Chaplain,* Weidenfeld and Nicolson, London 2003

De Unamuno, Miguel, *The Tragic Sense of Life*, Fontana, London 1962

Dillard, Annie, *Holy the Firm*, Harper and Row, New York 1984

Dostoevsky, Fyodor, *The Karamazov Brothers,* Oxford World's Classics 1998

Eliot, T.S., *The Complete Poems and Plays*, Harcourt Brace, New York 1952

Forster, Margaret, *Hidden Lives*, Penguin, London 1995

Freeman, Charles, *The Closing of the Western Mind,* Pimlico, London 2003

Freud, Sigmund, *Civilization, Society and Religion*, Penguin, London 1991

Gould, Stephen Jay, *I Have Landed*, Jonathan Cape, London 2002

Gray, John, *Straw Dogs*, Granta, London 2002

Grayling, A.C., *What is Good?* Weidenfeld and Nicolson, London 2003

Greenfield, Susan, *Tomorrow's People*, Penguin, London 2003

Hogg, James, *The Private Memoirs and Confessions of a Justified Sinner*, Canongate Classics, Edinburgh 1990

Holloway, Richard, *Godless Morality*, Canongate, Edinburgh 1999

Houellebecq, Michel, *Atomised*, Vintage, London 2001

Kramnick, Isaac (ed.), *The Portable Enlightenment Reader*, Penguin, New York 1995

Larkin, Philip, *Collected Poems*, Faber and Faber, London 1990

Lepp, Ignace, *Death and its Mysteries*, Burns and Oates, London 1969

MacNiece, Louis, *Collected Poems*, Faber and Faber, London 1991

Mill, John Stuart, *On Liberty*, Penguin Classics, London 1985

Morris, Jan, *Trieste and the Meaning of Nowhere*, Faber and Faber, London 2002

Nietzsche, Friedrich, *The Will to Power*, Vintage, New York 1968

Nietzsche, Friedrich, *Daybreak*, Cambridge University Press 1982

Nietzsche, Friedrich, *Basic Writings of Nietzsche*, tr. and ed. Walter Kaufman, The Modern Library, New York 1992

Ondaatje, Michael, *The English Patient*, Picador, London 1993

Rawls, John, *A Theory of Justice*, revised edition, Oxford University Press 1999

Rees, Martin, *Our Final Century*, Heinemann, London 2003

Tartt, Donna, *The Little Friend*, Bloomsbury, London 1992

Tessimond, A.S.J., *The Collected Poems*, ed. Hubert Nicholson, University of Reading Press, Reading 1985

Thomas, R.S., *Collected Poems*, Dent, London 1993

Updike, John, *Memories of the Ford Administration*, Penguin, London 1993

Weil, Simone, *Gravity and Grace*, Routledge & Kegan Paul, London 1987

Wheatcroft, Andrew, *Infidels*, Penguin Viking, London 2003

Permissions Acknowledgements

Extract from *Atomised* by Michel Houellebecq published by Heinemann. Used by permission of The Random House Group Limited.

Extract from 'Via Negativa', in *Collected Poems* by R. S. Thomas, published by JM Dent. Reproduced by permission.

'Psalm', in *Poems of Paul Celan* by Paul Celan, translated by Michael Hamburger, published by Anvil Press, 1995. Reproduced by permission.

Extract from *Hidden Lives*, copyright © Margaret Forster, 1995, reproduced by kind permission of the author and The Sayle Literary Agency, and of Penguin Books.

Extract from 'Road 1940', in *Selected Poems* by Sylvia Townsend Warner, published by Carcanet Press Limited, 1985. Reproduced by permission.

Excerpt from 'Little Gidding' in *Four Quartets*, copyright 1942 by T. S. Eliot and renewed 1970 by Esme Valerie Eliot, reprinted by permission of Harcourt, Inc.

Excerpt from 'Little Gidding' in *Four Quartets* in *Collected Poems 1909–1962* by T. S. Eliot, published by Faber and Faber. Reproduced by permission.